SWIMMING

Jonathan Wickes

2009

BOY SCOUTS OF AMERICA®

Note to the Counselor

Like other merit badges, the Swimming merit badge has been
developed to teach and train youth in a manner consistent with
the overall goals and values of the Boy Scouts of America. The
merit badge counselor should be fair and consistent and should
present and teach the skills as presented in this pamphlet. None
of the requirements should be omitted, and nothing should be
added to them.

Candidates with an extensive swimming background may
be able to meet all or most of the requirements with little or no
formal instruction from the counselor. Most Scouts, however,
will need instruction prior to completing the requirements.
Scouts may train as a single buddy pair or in small groups.
Training sessions can be on a flexible schedule. Alternatively,
larger groups may train together on a more formal basis at
prearranged times. A counselor may also provide individual
instruction as long as there is another adult or youth present.
Subject to equipment availability and other constraints, each
candidate should have the opportunity to choose which of the
optional requirements he will complete. The "Aquatics" section
of *Camp Program and Property Management* provides a sug-
gested outline for Swimming merit badge instruction.

The merit badge instruction should begin with a review of
requirement 3. This will lay a suitable foundation for safety and
first aid requirements 1 and 2. This review also will indicate individual levels of skill proficiency in various strokes, floating, and
feetfirst entry. Scouts should learn the leaping entry in the first
session. The leaping entry, the preferred entry for the swim tests
used in the Second and First Class rank requirements, should
be taught and emphasized in the first session as a safety skill to
be used throughout the class. The faceup float (requirement 6a)

35957
ISBN 978-0-8395-3352-8
©2008 Boy Scouts of America
2008 Printing

also should be taught in the First Class session as a confidence builder and as a resting and survival procedure for use during the class and beyond.

Stroke instruction should begin in the first session and continue throughout the course. Base individualized instruction on the proficiency of each participant. Each participant may be given the opportunity to complete the stroke requirement (requirement 5) when he appears ready.

Regarding other requirements, Scouts should first master surface dives (requirement 7) before beginning snorkeling and scuba diving (requirement 8a). They should receive diving instruction (requirement 9) prior to competitive skills instruction (requirement 8b). Survival skills and knowledge (requirements 4, 6b, 6c, and 6d) can be covered at any time, because they relate closely to the safety and preliminary skills in requirements 1 and 3.

If Scouts complete requirement 10 concurrently with in-water skills instruction, then the pertinent information should be presented early enough in the course to allow time for Scouts to study and prepare individual exercise program plans. Requirement 10c must be completed in writing. Requirements 10a, 10b, and 10d may be done orally, but Scouts should not simply listen to a presentation from the counselor. Each merit badge candidate must learn the material and demonstrate that knowledge by explaining the facts or concepts to his counselor.

Requirements

1. Discuss the prevention of and treatment for health concerns that could occur while swimming, including hypothermia, dehydration, sunburn, heat exhaustion, heatstroke, muscle cramps, hyperventilation, spinal injury, stings and bites, and cuts and scrapes.

2. Do the following:

    a. Identify the conditions that must exist before performing CPR on a person. Explain how to recognize such conditions.

    b. Demonstrate proper technique for performing CPR using a training device approved by your counselor.

3. Before doing the following requirements, successfully complete Second Class rank requirements 7a–7c and First Class rank requirements 9a–9c.

    Second Class rank requirements:

    (7a) Tell what precautions must be taken for a safe swim.

    (7b) Demonstrate your ability to jump feetfirst into water over your head in depth, level off and swim 25 feet on the surface, stop, turn sharply, resume swimming, then return to your starting place.

    (7c) Demonstrate water rescue methods by reaching with your arm or leg, by reaching with a suitable object, and by throwing lines and objects. Explain why swimming rescues should not be attempted when a reaching or throwing rescue is possible, and explain why and how a rescue swimmer should avoid contact with the victim.

First Class rank requirements:

(9a) Tell what precautions must be taken for a safe trip afloat.

(9b) Before doing the following requirement, successfully complete the BSA swimmer test:

Jump feetfirst into water over your head in depth, swim 75 yards in a strong manner using one or more of the following strokes: sidestroke, breaststroke, trudgen, or crawl; then swim 25 yards using an easy, resting backstroke. The 100 yards must be swum continuously and include at least one sharp turn. After completing the swim, rest by floating.

(9c) With a helper and a practice victim, show a line rescue both as tender and as rescuer. The practice victim should be approximately 30 feet from shore in deep water.

4. Demonstrate survival skills by jumping feetfirst into deep water wearing clothes (shoes, socks, swim trunks, long pants, belt, and long-sleeved shirt). Remove shoes and socks, inflate the shirt, and show that you can float using the shirt for support. Remove and inflate the pants. Swim 50 feet using the inflated pants for support, then show how to reinflate the pants while still afloat.

5. Swim continuously for 150 yards using the following strokes in good form and in a strong manner: front crawl or trudgen for 25 yards, back crawl for 25 yards, sidestroke for 25 yards, breaststroke for 25 yards, and elementary backstroke for 50 yards.

6. Do the following:

a. Float faceup in a resting position for at least one minute.

b. Demonstrate survival floating for at least five minutes.

c. While wearing a properly fitted personal flotation device (PFD), demonstrate the HELP and huddle positions. Explain their purposes.

d. Explain why swimming or survival floating will hasten the onset of hypothermia in cold water.

7. In water over your head, but not to exceed 10 feet, do each of the following:

   a. Use the feetfirst method of surface diving and bring an object up from the bottom.

   b. Do a headfirst surface dive (pike or tuck), and bring the object up again.

   c. Do a headfirst surface dive to a depth of at least 5 feet and swim underwater for three strokes. Come to the surface, take a breath, and repeat the sequence twice.

8. Do ONE of the following:

   a. Demonstrate snorkeling and scuba diving knowledge:

      (1) Demonstrate selection and fit of mask, snorkel, and fins; discuss safety in both pool and open-water snorkeling.

      (2) Demonstrate proper use of mask, snorkel, and fins for underwater search and rescue.

      (3) Describe the sport of scuba diving or snorkeling, and demonstrate your knowledge of BSA policies and procedures relating to that sport.

   OR

   b. Demonstrate the following competitive swimming skills:

      (1) Racing dive from a pool edge or dock edge (no elevated dives from racing platforms or starting blocks)

      (2) Racing form for 25 yards on one competitive stroke (front crawl, back crawl, breaststroke, or butterfly)

      (3) Racing turns for the stroke that you chose in 8b(2), OR, if the camp facilities cannot accommodate the racing turn, repeat 8b(2) with an additional stroke.

      (4) Describe the sport of competitive swimming.

9. Following the guidelines set in the BSA Safe Swim Defense, in water at least 7 feet deep, show a standing headfirst dive from a dock or pool deck. Show a long shallow dive, also from the dock or pool deck.

10. Do the following:

    a. Explain the health benefits of regular aerobic exercise, and explain why many people today do not get enough of the beneficial kinds of exercise.

    b. Discuss why swimming is favored as both a fitness and a therapeutic exercise.

    c. Write a plan for a swimming exercise program that will promote aerobic/vascular fitness, strength and muscle tone, body flexibility, and weight control for a person of Scout age. Identify resources and facilities available in your home community that would be needed for such a program.

    d. Discuss with your counselor the incentives and obstacles for staying with the fitness program you identified in requirement 10c. Explain the unique benefits that could be gained from this program, and discuss how personal health awareness and self-discipline would relate to your own willingness and ability to pursue such a program.

Contents

Safety

Developed more than 60 years ago, the procedures included in the Boy Scouts of America's water safety plan have earned Scouting what is believed to be the most commendable water safety record of any youth organization in the United States.

BSA Safe Swim Defense

All swimming activity in Scouting is conducted according to Safe Swim Defense standards. The eight points of Safe Swim Defense are as follows.

1. Qualified Supervision

All swimming activity must be supervised by a mature and conscientious adult age 21 or older who understands and knowingly accepts responsibility for the well-being and safety of those in his or her care, and who is trained in and committed to compliance with the eight points of BSA Safe Swim Defense. It is strongly recommended that all units have at least one adult or older youth member currently trained in BSA Swimming and Water Rescue or BSA Lifeguard to assist in the planning and conduct of all swimming activities.

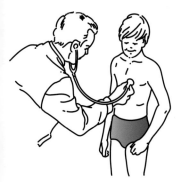

2. Personal Health Review

A complete health history is required of all participants as evidence of fitness for swimming activities. Forms for minors must be signed by a parent or legal guardian. Participants should be asked to relate any recent incidents of illness or injury just prior to the activity. Supervision and protection should be adjusted to anticipate any potential risks associated with individual health conditions. For significant health conditions, the adult supervisor should require an examination by a physician and consult with the parent, guardian, or caregiver for appropriate precautions.

3. Safe Area

All swimming areas must be carefully inspected and prepared for safety prior to each activity. Water depth, quality, temperature, movement, and clarity are important considerations. Hazards must be eliminated or isolated by conspicuous markings and discussed with participants.

Controlled access. There must be safe areas for all participating ability groups to enter and leave the water. Swimming areas of appropriate depth must be defined for each ability group. The entire area must be within easy reach of designated rescue personnel. The area must be clear of boat traffic, surfing, or other nonswimming activities.

Bottom conditions and depth: The bottom must be clear of trees and debris. Abrupt changes in depth are not allowed in the *nonswimmer* area. Isolated underwater hazards should be marked with floats. Rescue personnel must be able to easily reach the bottom. Maximum recommended water depth in clear water is 12 feet. Maximum water depth in turbid water is 8 feet.

Safe areas are best inspected as a team so hazards can be identified and removed if possible.

Visibility. Underwater swimming and diving are prohibited in turbid water. Turbid water exists when a swimmer treading water cannot see his feet. Swimming at night is allowed only in areas with both surface and underwater lighting.

Diving and elevated entry. Diving is permitted only into clear, unobstructed water from heights no greater than 40 inches. Water depth must be at least 7 feet for dives from fixed heights up to 18 inches and at least 10 feet for dives from the side or a diving board for heights from 18 inches to 40 inches. Persons should not jump into water from heights greater than they are tall, and only into water depths where impact with the bottom is absent or slight. No elevated entry is permitted where the person must clear any obstacle, including land.

Water temperature. Comfortable water temperature for swimming is near 80 degrees. Activity in water at 70 degrees or less should be of limited duration and closely monitored for negative effects of chilling.

Water quality. Bodies of stagnant, fetid water, areas with significant algae or foam, or areas polluted by livestock or waterfowl should be avoided. Comply with any signs posted by local health authorities. Swimming is not allowed in pools with green, murky, or cloudy water.

Moving water. Participants should be able to easily regain and maintain their footing in currents or waves. Areas with large waves, swiftly flowing currents, or moderate currents that flow toward the open sea or into areas of danger should be avoided.

Weather. Participants should be moved from the water to a position of safety whenever lightning or thunder threatens. Wait at least 30 minutes after the last lightning flash or thunder before leaving shelter. Take precautions to prevent sunburn, dehydration, and hypothermia.

PFD use. Swimming in clear water over 12 feet deep, in turbid water over 8 feet deep, or in flowing water may be allowed if all participants wear properly fitted personal flotation devices and the supervisor determines that swimming with PFDs is safe under the circumstances.

4. Response Personnel (Lifeguards)

Every swimming activity must be closely and continuously monitored by a trained rescue team on the alert for and ready to respond during emergencies. Professionally trained lifeguards satisfy this need when provided by a regulated facility or tour operator. When lifeguards are not provided by others, the adult supervisor must assign at least two rescue personnel, with additional numbers to maintain a ratio to participants of 1:10. The supervisor must provide instruction and rescue equipment and assign areas of responsibility as outlined in the BSA publication *Aquatics Supervision.* The qualified supervisor, the designated response personnel, and the lookout work together as a safety team. A simple emergency action plan should be formulated by the safety team and shared with participants as appropriate.

5. Lookout

The lookout continuously monitors the conduct of the swim, identifies any departures from Safe Swim Defense guidelines, alerts response personnel as needed, and monitors the weather and environment. The lookout should have a clear view of the entire area but be close enough for easy verbal communication. The lookout must have a sound understanding of *Safe Swim Defense* but is not required to perform rescues. The adult supervisor may serve simultaneously as the lookout but must assign the task to someone else if engaged in activities that preclude focused observation.

6. Ability Groups

All youth and adult participants are designated as *swimmers, beginners,* or *nonswimmers* based on swimming ability confirmed by standardized BSA swim classification tests. Each group is assigned a specific swimming area with depths consistent with those abilities. The classification tests should be renewed annually, preferably at the beginning of the season.

Swimmers pass this test: Jump feetfirst into water over the head in depth. Level off and swim 75 yards in a strong manner using one or more of the following strokes: sidestroke, breaststroke, trudgen, or crawl; then swim 25 yards using an easy resting backstroke. The 100 yards must be completed in one swim without stops and must include at least one sharp turn. After completing the swim, rest by floating.

Beginners pass this test: Jump feetfirst into water over the head in depth, level off, and swim 25 feet on the surface. Stop, turn sharply, resume swimming, and return to the starting place.

Anyone who has not completed either the *beginner* or *swimmer* tests is classified as a *nonswimmer.*

The *nonswimmer* area should be no more than waist to chest deep and should be enclosed by physical boundaries such as the shore, a pier, or lines. The enclosed *beginner* area should contain water of standing depth and may extend to depths just over the head. The *swimmer* area may be up to 12 feet in depth in clear water and should be defined by floats or other markers.

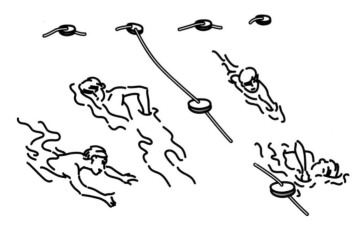

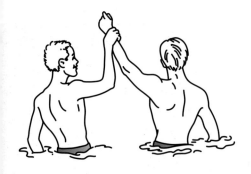

7. Buddy System

Every participant is paired with another participant. Buddies stay together, monitor each other, and alert the safety team if either needs assistance or is missing.

Buddies check into and out of the area together. Buddies are normally in the same ability group and remain in their assigned area. If they are not of the same ability group, then they swim in the area assigned to the buddy with the lesser ability.

Buddy checks indicate how closely the buddies are keeping track of each other. Roughly every 10 minutes, or as needed to keep the buddies together, the lookout, or other person designated by the supervisor, gives an audible signal, such as a single whistle blast, and a call for "Buddies." Buddies are expected to raise each other's hand before completion of a slow, audible count to 10. Buddies who take longer to find each other should be reminded of their responsibility for each other's safety.

A buddy check also helps the safety team monitor everyone in the water. If a buddy is missing, a search is begun immediately in accordance with a prearranged emergency action plan. If everyone has a buddy, a count is made by area and compared with the total number known to be in the water. Once the count is confirmed, a signal is given to resume swimming.

8. Discipline

Rules are effective only when followed. All participants should know, understand, and respect the rules and procedures for safe swimming provided by Safe Swim Defense guidelines. Applicable rules should be discussed prior to the outing and reviewed for all participants at the water's edge just before the swimming activity begins. People are more likely to follow directions when they know the reasons for rules and procedures. Consistent, impartially applied rules supported by skill and good judgment provide stepping-stones to a safe, enjoyable outing.

Pool and Surf Swimming

Safe Swim Defense applies to swimming at a beach, private or public pool, wilderness pond, stream, lake, or anywhere Scouts swim. Here are some additional points for the pool and the surf.

Pool. If the swimming activity is in a public facility where others are using the pool at the same time and the pool operator provides guard personnel, there may be no need for additional Scout lifeguards and lookouts. However, there must always be an adult supervisor who understands his or her responsibility and ensures that the elements of Safe Swim Defense are followed. The buddy system is also critically important, even in a public pool. Even in a crowd, you are alone without protection if no one is paying attention to your circumstances.

The rule that people swim only in water depths suited to their ability also applies at pools. Most public pools divide shallow and deep water. This may be enough for defining appropriate swimming areas. If not, the supervisor should clearly point out to participants the appropriate areas of the public facility.

Surf. The surf environment—with its wave action, currents, tides, backwash, and sea life such as stinging jellyfish—requires precautions for safe swimming that aren't necessary in other environments. A swimmer's physical condition and skill are very important and should enable the swimmer to recover footing in waves, swim for long periods without getting worn out, and remain calm and in control when faced with unexpected conditions.

Designated swimming areas are marked by flags or pennants that are easy to see. Beginners and nonswimmers should be positioned inshore from standing lifeguards who are equipped with rescue equipment. Better swimmers are permitted seaward of the lifeguards but must remain shoreward of anchored marker buoys. The lifeguard-to-swimmer ratio should always be 1-to-10 with a rescue team supplied with a rescue tube or other flotation aid stationed at the beach area.

Unless your unit is experienced in ocean swimming, it is probably best to swim at a beach with professional lifeguards.

Rip Currents

The United States Lifesaving Association estimates that most rescues—about 80 percent—at surf beaches involve swimmers caught in rip currents. More than 100 swimmers die each year from this swimming hazard. Rip currents are long, narrow sections of water that form after waves break and the water goes back out. Rip currents form a funnel of current that moves much faster than the current on either side. The current can be so strong that it may be difficult or impossible to swim against it. It can carry an unsuspecting swimmer long distances from shore and even out to sea.

Rip currents occur in oceans and any place where there are waves, including bodies of water such as the Great Lakes. To avoid getting caught in a rip current, do not swim near piers or jetties (walls built out into the water to protect a harbor or beach). Rip currents are often hard to see, but look for the following clues:

- An area having a noticeable difference in water color

- A channel of churning, choppy water

- A line of foam, seaweed, or debris moving steadily away from shore

- A break in the incoming wave pattern

If you are caught in a rip current, don't fight it by swimming toward the beach. Instead, turn and escape by swimming parallel to the shore. If that doesn't work, float or tread water. Call or wave for help.

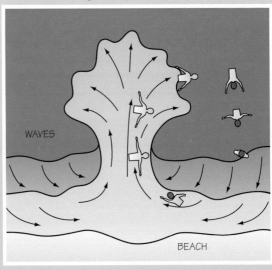

First Aid

Following Safe Swim Defense will eliminate any serious risks in swimming, but be prepared for minor injuries and remember to take proper precautions.

Hypothermia occurs when the body's core temperature falls below the normal range and the body loses heat faster than it can produce it. Early signs of heat loss include bluish lips and shivering. Further cooling will upset the victim's ability to think clearly and to do simple tasks. The person may appear groggy and lack coordination. As cooling continues, the pulse rate slows and blood is directed to the critical organs and away from the extremities as the body attempts to prevent further heat loss. The heart and lungs keep working at the expense of the hands, feet, and brain. Further cooling will lead to unconsciousness and even death.

The first treatment for hypothermia is to prevent further heat loss. Once out of the water, the victim should not be allowed to walk. Move him to warmth and shelter such as a building, tent, or vehicle. As soon as possible, remove wet clothing and put on dry clothes or wrap the person in a blanket or dry towels. If the victim is unconscious, open the airway and check for breathing. You may apply warm (but not hot) towels or items such as hot water bottles wrapped in a towel to *only* the trunk, crotch, neck, and head. Do not rub his legs or apply warming devices to the arms or legs. These actions may cause more blood to flow to the surface of the skin and away from vital organs. Finally, since even mild cases of hypothermia place the body in a highly stressed condition, closely watch all hypothermia victims for several hours even if they appear to have recovered.

Heat reactions, including heat exhaustion and heatstroke, result when the body can't keep itself cool enough. Symptoms of *heat exhaustion* may include dizziness, faintness, nausea, and a severe lack of energy. A person with heat exhaustion also may develop a headache, muscle cramps, and a rapid pulse; look pale; and be sweating heavily. To treat heat exhaustion, have the victim lie down in a cool, shady spot with the feet raised. Loosen clothing and cool him with a damp cloth or a fan. Have him sip water. Recovery should be rapid. If the condition worsens, get medical help.

Prevent heat reactions by drinking plenty of fluids and limiting time out in the open on hot days.

Heatstroke is the extreme, life-threatening stage of a heat reaction in which *dehydration* (water loss) has caused a very high body temperature. The victim's cooling system has started to fail, and the person's core temperature is at a dangerously high level. In addition to any symptoms of heat exhaustion, heatstroke symptoms can include hot, sweaty, red skin, confusion, and disorientation; the victim may be unconscious. The victim must be cooled immediately. Loosen tight clothing, fan him, and apply wet towels. If you have ice packs, wrap them in a thin barrier (such as a T-shirt) and place them under the armpits and against the neck and groin area. If the person is able to drink, give small amounts of cool water. Treat for shock and seek emergency medical help.

Muscle cramps, sometimes called muscle spasms, occur when muscles are not getting enough oxygen or nutrients or when the blood flow cannot prevent the build-up of wastes in muscles. Vigorous exercise and sweating can cause muscle cramps in the limbs. Cold water or cold weather increases the likelihood of cramping. Sudden, vigorous exercise without proper warm-up also can increase the risk of muscle cramps. If a muscle begins to cramp while you are swimming, get out of the water and massage the cramp. If conditions are hot, cool down and drink fluids. If conditions are cold, find warmth and cover. Rub the cramping muscles to improve circulation.

Sunburn is a familiar condition that can occur during swimming activities. Reflected sunlight from the water can be as damaging as direct exposure. To prevent sunburn, cover up, use a waterproof sunscreen, and limit your time in the sun. If your skin begins to redden or feel painful, get out of the sun. To treat sunburn, apply clean, wet compresses (cloths, towels, or gauze pads) dipped in cool water. Protect the burned area from further sun exposure.

Stings and bites are not a common hazard when swimming in pools or lakes, but in saltwater swimmers may suffer severe stings from certain types of jellyfish or other saltwater creatures. Knowing the body of water you are swimming in and avoiding possible contact with dangerous sea animals is the best strategy. *For jellyfish stings,* soak the area with vinegar or alcohol, or cover with a paste of baking soda mixed with water. Get medical help if the pain is severe; if the pain does not let up in a short

If you have a cramp while swimming in deep water and cannot swim to safety, float on your back or survival float and wait for help.

time; or if the victim has an allergic reaction, feels dizzy, or has trouble breathing. *For typical insect stings and bites,* apply basic first aid as described in the *Boy Scout Handbook* or the *First Aid* merit badge pamphlet.

Cuts and scrapes may occur on the feet when swimming in natural waters if the bottom has not been carefully checked for hazards. In pool swimming, such injuries are more likely when climbing in and out of the water without being careful along rough edges or corners. As in other situations, the wound should be cleaned, disinfected, and covered. The patrol first-aid kit should contain appropriate supplies for minor wound treatment. For severe bleeding injuries, control bleeding with direct pressure or at pressure points until emergency medical help arrives.

Spinal injuries can occur from diving into shallow or obstructed water. Rescuers must be very careful when a spinal injury is suspected. Spinal injuries can be fatal or can cause paralysis. If the victim is not handled properly, additional serious injury could result. Moving a victim is an extremely delicate task best left to trained emergency personnel, but if no one else is present you may need to act. In a swimming accident, you may have to move the victim to prevent drowning or to perform rescue breathing.

Speaking of stings and bites, if you will be swimming in the ocean, beware of sharks. (Although bull sharks have been known to inhabit the waterways of the Mississippi!) The possibility of a shark bite is pretty remote, but play it safe by finding out what you can about the area where you will be swimming before you decide to dive in.

Cardiopulmonary resuscitation (CPR) is the important first response in a cardiac emergency. CPR is used in near-drownings when a victim's breathing **and** heartbeat have stopped. Include individuals trained in CPR at every swimming outing. Complete CPR should be attempted only by persons trained and qualified under the supervision of a trained instructor. The *Boy Scout Handbook* and the *First Aid* merit badge pamphlet further explain CPR and when it should be used.

Some important techniques are not covered by requirement 2 of the Swimming merit badge. To receive full and proper CPR training, contact your American Red Cross chapter or the American Heart Association. See the resources section at the end of this pamphlet. Your counselor can help you.

When tending to a suspected spinal injury victim, move the victim's head, neck, and back as little as possible. The technique used to limit this movement is called *in-line stabilization.* For information on this technique, see the chapter concerning spinal injury management in the *Lifesaving* merit badge pamphlet.

Hyperventilation is the result of overbreathing, either deliberately or as a result of panic. Hyperventilating decreases the level of carbon dioxide in the blood and suppresses the breathing reflex. The likely result is dizziness and fainting. Hyperventilation from panic is not likely to occur in swimming if all participants stay in water suited to their individual skill levels and the activity is properly supervised and disciplined. If a swimmer becomes panicky, he or she should be removed from the water and calmed. Before resuming any water activity, determine and resolve the cause of the panic. A foolish swimmer may deliberately hyperventilate to suppress the breathing reflex for underwater swimming. This is dangerous and puts the swimmer at high risk. Such conduct is prohibited and should be sharply disciplined.

Survival Skills

Cold Water

Moving water and wind substantially increase the loss of body heat. Swimming and treading water also cool the body faster than remaining still.

When a person is in cold water, the skin and nearby tissues cool quickly. The body immediately begins producing heat to rewarm the skin and to prevent the cooling of vital organs. Hypothermia occurs when the body loses heat faster than it can produce it, which causes the internal body temperature to decrease.

Water or air temperature lower than 70 degrees poses hypothermia risks. If goose bumps appear on wet skin shortly after leaving the water, then the air temperature should be considered cold and swimmers should take proper precautions. The first protection for cold-water activity is to reduce the length of time in or on the water. At 70 degrees, maximum safe in-the-water time is approximately 20 minutes. Open-water swimming in temperatures of 65 degrees or lower may pose substantial risks and should be avoided. In all swimming activities, precautions should include procedures and equipment for immediate warming of anyone showing symptoms of chill.

Activities Afloat

For all activity afloat on cold water or in cold weather, wear appropriate clothing to keep you warm. You should wear a personal flotation device (PFD) at all times, normally on top of the outermost garment. Have a dry change of clothes available in case of a spill. As in swimming, preparation and plans for any activity afloat should include procedures and equipment for warming anyone showing symptoms of chill. Overboard activity is not recommended in water temperatures of 65 degrees or lower, except for closely supervised capsize skills training in preparation for activity afloat.

A properly fitted U.S. Coast Guard–approved PFD should be worn for all activities afloat in small craft. The PFD will help keep you afloat. In addition, it can provide insulation and significantly reduce heat loss in cold water that could lead to hypothermia.

If you are alone in cold water and more than a short distance from safety, your best strategy is to float motionless. This will help you conserve heat. Keep your PFD and all clothing on for insulation. Heat loss is most rapid from the head and crotch.

Because water will move heat away from the body faster than air, keeping your face and head in the water will speed up heat loss. Vigorous swimming will chill you most rapidly. Treading water is tiring and will produce heat loss almost as rapidly as swimming. Survival floating, or drown-proofing (described later in this chapter), might be somewhat better than swimming or treading water if your movements are slow and limited, but submerging the head and face will increase heat loss.

For treading water, you can use the rotary kick, but do so sparingly. Your body will tire quickly and lose heat rapidly when treading water.

HELP (heat escape lessening posture)

Huddle together with sides touching.

For these reasons, your best cold-water survival strategy is to float motionless with your PFD and clothes on, your head out of the water, and your legs drawn up close to your chest. This is called the *heat escape lessening posture* (HELP). If you are stranded in cold water with one or more persons, you should huddle together to reduce the cold-water contact and conserve heat. To do this, press together tightly and float motionless.

Surviving in Cold Water

- Wear a PFD.

- Keep your head out of the water.

- Get out of the water onto your boat, a log, a raft, or anything that floats.

- Remain as still as possible while in the water.

- While afloat in the water, do not attempt to swim unless it is to reach a nearby craft, fellow survivor, or floating object that you can lean on or climb onto.

- If there is more than one person in the water, huddling is recommended while waiting to be rescued.

- Maintain a positive mental attitude. Never give up hope.

Survival floating, or drown-proofing

Survival Floating

What if you find yourself in deep water without flotation support and too far from shore to swim? Perhaps you were swept out to sea by an unusually strong current or thrown overboard from a boat in strong waves. You must keep yourself afloat until help arrives. Floating on your back is a good plan if there are no waves. Another possibility is survival floating, or drown-proofing, which will work even if you are being tossed around by wind and waves.

To survival float, begin by taking a breath, putting your face in the water, and floating facedown in a relaxed position (the jellyfish float). For most people, the back of the neck will break the surface of the water. After holding your breath for a comfortable length of time, begin to exhale slowly while spreading your legs and bringing your arms up near the surface. As you exhale, bring your legs together and push gently down with your arms. This movement should give you just enough lift to raise your head and mouth above the surface for a quick breath. After getting your breath, lower your head and immediately return to your relaxed, facedown position.

Several different arm and leg movements (such as an occasional slow scissors kick) may work well when survival floating. Experiment and practice to find what works best for you. Remember: Less movement is better because you are trying to conserve your energy. Slow, relaxed movement is better than quick or precise movements that take more energy.

As you practice survival floating, you may find that you need to keep your head above water longer than one quick inhalation and that you end up briefly treading water. This will quickly tire you. To correct the problem, be sure to exhale completely while your head is down in the water. Practice survival floating until it becomes easy for you to make slow movements and to exhale in the water and lift your head just enough for one quick breath. Remember to relax—it may be a long wait.

Clothing Inflation

Occasionally, a boater or passenger will fall into deep water far from shore. If this ever happens to you, being able to inflate (fill with air) a shirt or a pair of pants is a survival skill that could save your life. These items of clothing can help you stay afloat while you swim to safety or until you are rescued.

There are several skills used to inflate clothing. While inflating your clothes, you may have to tread water by using the scissors kick or whip kick, but this may soon tire you. If you become tired before your clothes can be inflated, you must be able to rest by floating on your back as well as in a facedown survival float.

If you fall into the water wearing a button-up shirt made of cotton or some other tightly woven fabric, you can stay afloat by trapping air in the shirt's back and shoulders. (A shirt without a collar does not work well for flotation.) Button the top collar button or hold the collar closed with your hand. Open a space between the second and third buttons. Position your head so that your mouth is over the opening and then blow air into it. Hold the collar tight and keep your elbows down to prevent air leakage.

Step 1—Inflate a pocket.

A pair of pants can provide additional flotation. While wearing the inflated shirt, first remove your shoes, letting them sink or float free. You don't need to worry about your socks. Then remove your pants carefully. Do not turn them inside out. Inflate a pocket with a puff of air. The pocket will support the pants while you carry out the next steps. It will also keep them from sinking if they slip out of your hands. Next, use a square knot to tie the pant legs together as near to the bottom of the pants as you can. Pull the knot tight and close the fly.

"Splashing" air into the pants is the quickest and easiest means of inflation, but it might take some practice before you master this technique. Hold the waistband open just below the surface, cup your hand in the air, and strike the water just in front of the pants. Follow through so that the air pushed down by your hand enters the opening of the pants. You should move the air just

Step 2—Splash air into the pants.

below the surface and then sideways so that it bubbles upward into the pants. The method will not work if you fail to lift your hand clear of the water or if you strike directly downward. If you have difficulty with this method, you can fill the pants by holding the waistband under the water with both hands, taking a breath, sinking so that your mouth is lower than the waistband and then blowing air into them from beneath.

When the pants are inflated, grasp the waist with the fly toward you and place your head through the opening between the legs. Rest your head on the knot, lie back, and relax. If you have a belt, you can use it in several ways. In one method, you close the belt (if not already closed), grasp it in front of the fly, pull down to bunch the belt loops, and tighten the waist. Insert your leg through the loop formed by the excess in the belt. The other way is to slide both ends of the belt out of the front belt loops, so that it passes through the back loops only. Place the front of the pants next to your chest and fasten the

Step 3—Place the pants around your neck.

belt behind you. Doing this frees up your hands for signaling or slowly swimming the elementary backstroke. Air will escape from the pants if you allow the material to dry. Splash water over them from time to time to help them stay filled with air. As needed, add air to the pants by loosening the waistband and splashing in air.

Swimming Skills

One of the most important elements of safety in the water is the ability to swim. Strong swimmers can swim a reasonable distance with a confident, steady stroke. But strong swimmers are not safe swimmers until they can make a safe water entry, swim a restful stroke, and maintain themselves in the water when hurt or exhausted.

Every First Class Scout has demonstrated that he is a strong, safe swimmer who has mastered certain in-water skills. The BSA swimmer test—required for First Class advancement—includes these in-water skills and represents the minimum level of ability for safe deepwater swimming. Consider the components of the test:

1. "Jump feetfirst into water over your head in depth, . . ."

You must be able to make an abrupt entry into deep water and begin swimming without any aids. Walking in from shallow water, easing in from the edge or down a ladder, pushing off from a pool's side or bottom, and gaining forward momentum by diving do not satisfy this requirement.

2. ". . . swim 75 yards in a strong manner using one or more of the following strokes: sidestroke, breaststroke, trudgen, or crawl; . . ."

You must be able to cover distance with a strong, confident stroke. The 75 yards must not be the outer limit of your ability. You should be able to complete the distance and still have enough stamina to avoid undue risks. Dog paddling and strokes repeatedly interrupted and restarted are insufficient, and underwater swimming is not allowed. The strokes listed above may include variations. Any strong sidestroke or breaststroke, or any strong overarm stroke—including the back crawl—is acceptable.

3. ". . . then swim 25 yards using an easy, resting backstroke. . . ."

You must perform a restful, free-breathing backstroke that can be used to avoid exhaustion during swimming activity. This part of the test will need to follow a more strenuous swimming activity to show that you can, in fact, use the backstroke to rest and recover. You must accomplish the change of stroke in deep water without any push-off or other aid. Any variation of the elementary backstroke is acceptable. An overarm back crawl may be used if it clearly allows you to rest and catch your breath.

4. ". . . The 100 yards must be swum continuously and include at least one sharp turn. . . ."

You must cover the total distance without stopping. The sharp turn demonstrates your ability to reverse direction in deep water without assistance or a push-off from the side or bottom.

5. ". . . After completing the swim, rest by floating."

This critically important part of the test evaluates your ability to maintain yourself in the water indefinitely even though exhausted or otherwise unable to keep swimming. Treading water or swimming in place will further tire you and therefore is unacceptable. The length of the float test is not important, except that it must be long enough for the tester to determine that you are resting and likely could continue to do so for a prolonged period. Drown-proofing may be sufficient if it is clearly restful, but it is not preferred. If the test is completed except for the floating requirement, you may be retested on the floating (after instruction) only if the tester feels confident that you can initiate the float when exhausted.

Entering the Water

Get into the habit of entering the water feetfirst whenever you practice swimming skills. This will protect your head and neck from being injured by unseen objects below the surface or when the water is shallower than you think. It is always safer to learn and practice entries in water that is over your head in depth.

3 FEET MAXIMUM

Leaping entry (stride jump)

Leaping Entry (Stride Jump)

Stand with both feet near the edge of the pier or pool. The water should be at least 5 feet deep. Lean forward and step far out over the water while pushing off with the other foot. Keep your arms straight and slightly to the side. Keep your head up by looking forward. You should lean into and move out over the water, not jump up. Limit the height of the starting point to 3 feet above the water. As your feet and legs enter the water, snap them together as in a scissors kick. Bring your arms straight down in a slapping motion to break your entry into the water. Timing is key; if you do it right, you won't even get your chin wet. In lifesaving, this entry allows you to keep your subject constantly in sight.

Floating

Whenever you are floating, try to keep your lungs well inflated with air. This will help you remain buoyant.

Floating faceup is the most restful way to maintain yourself in deep water. This simple skill requires buoyancy and balance. Buoyancy is the ability to float. Your body has two balancing points known as the *center of buoyancy* and the *center of weight*. When you are floating, your body's center of buoyancy is in your chest. The air in your lungs is mainly what keeps you afloat. Your body's center of weight is lower—about the level of your hips. Your hips and legs are quite heavy, because they are made of muscle and bone. In the water, gravity pulls your hips and legs down, while the air in your lungs makes the upper part of your body more buoyant. When you try to float on your back, your legs and feet sink and your head and chest rise.

To float without moving, you need to adjust your body so that the center of buoyancy is directly above the center of weight. For many people, this means floating with the feet well below the surface and only the head or mouth at the water's surface. When floating, some swimmers are positioned almost vertically in the water.

It is possible to float in a more horizontal position. You cannot change your center of buoyancy, because you cannot change the position of your lungs. You can, however, change your center of weight. To change your center of weight when floating, move your arms away from your sides and above your head. Bend your legs at the knees and let your feet sink or pull your feet up behind and underneath you. This will shift your center of weight closer to your center of buoyancy.

Practice floating in chest-deep water. Start from a standing position. Take a deep breath and hold it. Bend your knees slightly and lean backward, arching your back and moving your neck backward until your ears are in the water and your chin is your highest point. Slowly move your hands and arms away from your sides with your palms up. Keep your arms and hands in the water and move them so they form a Y above your shoulders. Do not try to arm stroke or kick into a higher position, because this will throw off your balance. Relax and let your body settle into its natural floating level and position in the water.

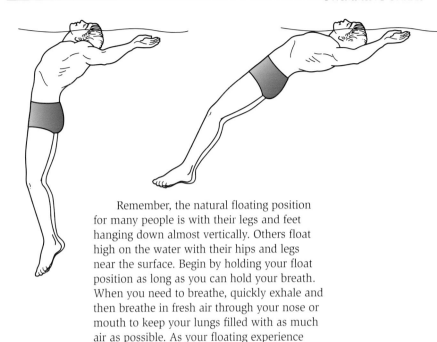

Remember, the natural floating position for many people is with their legs and feet hanging down almost vertically. Others float high on the water with their hips and legs near the surface. Begin by holding your float position as long as you can hold your breath. When you need to breathe, quickly exhale and then breathe in fresh air through your nose or mouth to keep your lungs filled with as much air as possible. As your floating experience and confidence increase, you will be able to breathe in a more relaxed and natural rhythm.

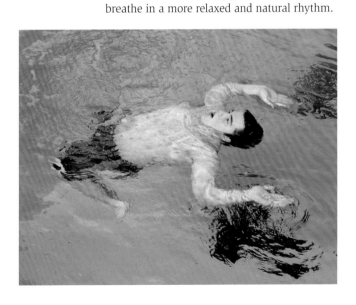

Swimming Strokes

By completing the Second Class and First Class swimming requirements, you have shown that you have some skill and endurance. To earn the Swimming merit badge you must further demonstrate your swimming strength and stroke proficiency by swimming 150 yards using a combination of five strokes. You must swim continuously in a strong manner for the entire distance and show good form on the front crawl or trudgen for 25 yards, the back crawl for 25 yards, the sidestroke for 25 yards, the breaststroke for 25 yards, and the elementary backstroke for 50 yards.

"Good form" means that you need to perform each stroke with the technique described in this pamphlet. For example, the breaststroke is a restful stroke that includes a long, prone glide between strokes. If your breaststroke is a vigorous, bobbing stroke as used in competition, it is not satisfactory for this requirement. Doing the backstroke using a frog kick rather than a whip kick also is unacceptable for this requirement.

You also are required to swim the specified strokes in a "strong manner." This means no rest stops and no gasping, panting finishes. The stroke sequence begins with the more strenuous strokes and moves through to the more restful strokes, with the last stroke being the most restful. *You should follow the stroke sequence as presented in the requirement.* If you complete the swim "in a strong manner" in the specified sequence, then you should be rested and able to continue well beyond the 150-yard requirement.

On the following pages, you will find the required strokes illustrated and explained as you should swim them to complete requirement 5.

Front Crawl

The front crawl has three parts: the flutter kick, the rotating arm stroke, and rhythmic breathing. It is the fastest and one of the most graceful of all swimming strokes.

In competition, the crawl stroke is called "freestyle."

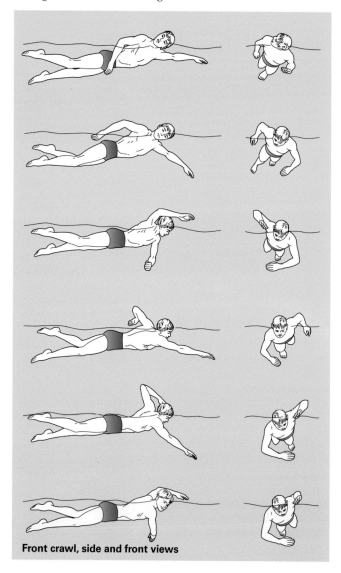

Front crawl, side and front views

Kick. The flutter kick relies on relaxed ankles and the use of the entire leg. The movement begins at the hips and flows to the feet. As one foot moves downward, the other comes up in a beating, or fluttering, rhythm. Kick from the hip and thigh, not from the knee. During the downward part of the kick, your ankle stays relaxed and your knee is slightly bent. As your foot reaches the end of the kick, straighten your leg and allow your foot to snap downward. As your foot moves upward, keep that leg and knee straight.

Flutter kick

The kick should be smooth and steady, and your feet should stay just under the water with only your heels breaking the surface. The distance between your feet is usually only about 8 to 12 inches. The number of kicks, or beats, during one complete arm cycle can vary. For swimming short distances, six kicks per arm cycle works well. You can practice the kick by holding the edge of the pool or by supporting yourself on a kickboard.

Arm Stroke. Most of the forward motion of the front crawl comes from the arm stroke. After diving or pushing off on your stomach with your arms out in front of you, begin the arm stroke with your hands just below the surface. Keep your hands relaxed with your fingers straight. The water level should be between your eyebrows and your hairline. Look forward and slightly down so you can see where you are going. Avoid looking straight down or bobbing your head up and down.

The arm stroke has three phases: catch, power, and recovery—or CPR. To begin the catch, slightly bend your right wrist and elbow as you move the entire arm downward. Have your palm facing away from your body. Keep your elbow, hand, and wrist fixed in this position. Your hand should be directly in line with your shoulder.

The catch phase of the arm stroke is called the "catch" because it feels like your palm and upper arm have grabbed hold of something.

For the power phase, straighten your wrist and bend the elbow so your forearm is about 45 degrees from the upper arm. Point your fingers down and inward. Push hard against the water, and sweep your hand and forearm down and back under your chest. Your hand will pass just a few inches from the centerline of your body. Your palm should be flat and should push backward against the water. As your hand becomes level with your shoulder, begin to straighten out your arm as it continues to move back and out to just beside your right hip. Your upper body will roll, with your left hip turning down and toward the centerline. This turns your right hip up toward the top of the water just as your right hand reaches the end of the power phase.

As your hand exits the water, the recovery phase begins. Start by lifting your elbow up and forward. Keep your wrist and hand relaxed and trailing behind or hanging below your elbow. As your hand passes the shoulder, it reaches up and forward to enter the water again when it is at shoulder level. When your fingertips are even with your eye and your arm is straightened to about three-quarters of its length, allow your fingertips to smoothly enter the water. Rotate your hand so that your thumb enters first as your arm straightens under the water to its full length.

The "Catch-Up" Style

For many recreational swimmers the arms are always in opposite positions when they do the front crawl. That is, as the right hand exits the water at the hip, the left hand enters the water and moves into the catch position. While one arm is in the power phase, the other arm is in the recovery phase. However, some recreational swimmers leave the forward arm straight while the recovering arm "catches up." In other words, the recovering arm enters the water while the other arm is just beginning the power phase, instead of when the power phase is nearly complete. Both arms are briefly forward of the head. When swimming at a relaxed place, the "catch-up" style allows a short glide in a streamlined position.

Breathing and Coordination. Swimmers doing the front crawl use a breathing rhythm of one breath for every one, two, three, or more arm cycles. For the purpose of learning and demonstrating the front crawl, you should take a breath for every set of arm cycles on the same side. During the previous arm cycles, slowly exhale through your nose and mouth.

When you need to take a breath, exhale all of the remaining air into the water during the power phase of the arm stroke. As your body rotates during the middle of the power phase, start turning your head so that your mouth is out of the water just as your hand exits by your hip. At the beginning of the recovery phase, inhale quickly and return your head to its former position. Take a breath every arm cycle until you can do it without having to pause. When the stroke is performed correctly, a wave will form around your head as you turn to breathe. Your mouth will be located in the trough of the wave.

Back Crawl

The back crawl, or backstroke, has two parts: a flutter kick and a continuous arm stroke. There is no rhythmic breathing since the face and mouth are above the water.

Kick. The back crawl kick is similar to the front crawl flutter kick but is done deeper in the water. The legs alternate, with the upward kick being the most forceful. Your ankles remain flexible and your toes point away from your head at all times. This allows your feet to function like divers' fins. On the downward part of the kick, keep your leg and knee straight. For the upward part of the kick, bend your knee and kick from the hip as if you were punting a football with the top of your foot. When your knee is just a few inches below the surface, stop the upward motion of the thigh and straighten the knee and leg. Remember to keep your ankles relaxed, so your feet will respond to the water pressure as your legs move.

Arm Stroke. The arm stroke for the back crawl involves alternating the arms, much like the front crawl arm stroke. You can start the arm stroke by pushing off on your back with both arms at your side and then lifting one arm out of the water, keeping it straight. As your arm moves back toward your head, roll a little onto the same side and drop your shoulder a bit deeper in the water. Your hand should enter the water little finger first. Your palm should face out and your wrist should be slightly bent. Allow your hand to slice down into the water until it is 8 to 12 inches below the surface. Your hand is now in the catch position. At the same time, start lifting your other arm out of the water for its recovery phase so that it will enter the water when the first arm has finished the power phase.

Back crawl, side and front views

The back crawl can be used for recreational swimming and in competition.

The key to the power phase of the arm stroke is bending your elbow and pushing against the water with your hand toward your feet. Do not try to keep your arm straight, which will either pull it to the side of your body or up toward the surface. As your hand moves from the catch position, begin to bend your elbow so that it points toward the bottom of the lake or pool. Keep your elbow bent and pull directly toward your feet with your entire arm. In the water, keep your hand higher than your elbow. About halfway through the power phase, your elbow will be bent 90 degrees and your hand will move toward the surface of the water.

The second half of the power phase involves using your hand to push the water toward your hip and straightening out your arm. At the very end of the power phase, flip your hand downward as it passes your thigh. Your palm will be facing the bottom and your arm will be fully straightened. This downward motion of the hand will cause your body to roll to the opposite side just as your other hand is entering the water. This raises your shoulder to make it easier to recover the arm while the opposite shoulder goes deeper into the water for its catch position.

The recovery phase is intended to give the arm muscles a rest. Begin by lifting your arm straight up in the air so your thumb and back of your hand leave the water first. Relax your hand, wrist, arm, and back muscles, but do not bend your elbow. Move your arm in a half-circle motion. The opposite arm will follow the same pattern, beginning its pull as your body rolls toward that side to begin the recovery of the first arm. Your arms are directly opposite each other at all times.

Breathing and Coordination. Body position is important for the back crawl. Be sure to keep your hips up and avoid a partial sitting position. Your head should be back with your ears in the water. Avoid turning your head from side to side, because your head position serves to anchor and steady the entire stroke. To coordinate arm and leg movements, count a six-beat kick (each upward leg kick is one beat) and complete one full arm cycle in six beats. In other words, one arm should enter the water on the count of one, and the opposite arm should enter the water on the count of four. Although the back crawl is a free-breathing stroke, you should develop a breathing rhythm that feels comfortable to you. The simplest pattern is to inhale when one arm recovers and exhale when the other arm recovers.

Sidestroke

The sidestroke is a good long-distance stroke with a long, restful glide. It also introduces the scissors kick, which is used in swimming rescues. The scissors kick is mainly responsible for the forward motion of the stroke.

Kick. The scissors kick is a powerful kick that provides a resting period between arm strokes. To do the scissors kick, bring your knees together and then bend them as you bring your lower legs and heels toward the buttocks. Without pausing, move your legs into the catch position. Move your top leg forward and your bottom leg back until your legs and knees are straight. To move into the power phase, bring both legs back together with a force ful snapping motion like closing a pair of scissors. Keep your legs together during the glide position with the toes pointed back.

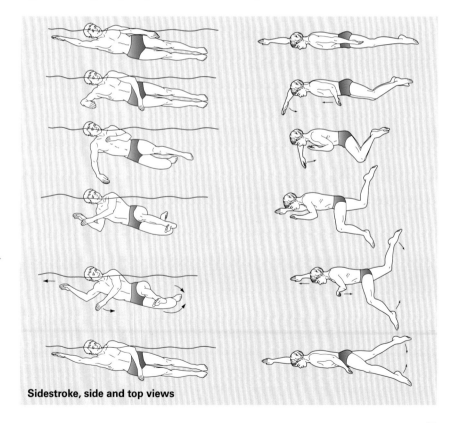

Sidestroke, side and top views

Arm Stroke. Start in the glide position on your side with one ear in the water and the nose, mouth, and other ear out of the water. With your body on its side, straighten the leading (bottom) arm to its full length with your ear resting on your shoulder and your palm facedown. The trailing (top) arm should rest comfortably alongside your body with the hand above the thigh. Turn the palm of the leading arm from facing down until it is vertical with the thumb on top. Begin moving the leading arm into a catch position by moving the hand in a downward direction toward the feet.

The power phase is a pull with the hand just below the top of the water and the elbow bent. Move your leading arm until it reaches the middle of your chest, while you move your trailing arm up the side of your body. Both hands should arrive at the same time in front of the upper chest. The trailing arm begins its catch and power phases while the leading arm recovers by moving back into the glide position. Reach out straight out from your shoulder with the trailing arm. Use your hand and arm to push the water toward your feet while they move to the side of your body. Keep both arms straight during the glide, or resting phase of the stroke.

Breathing and Coordination. In the sidestroke, the arm strokes and scissors kick are combined so that the legs are drawn up as the leading and trailing arms move toward the chest. To help coordinate your arms and legs in the sidestroke, remember the phrase, "pull, kick, glide." Start by moving your legs into the catch position. With your trailing arm straight and your legs apart for the scissors kick, the power phases for both the trailing arm and kick begin and end at the same time. During this time the leading arm recovers to the glide position. When you have finished both the kick and trailing arm stroke, rest and relax your muscles. Hold the glide position for three or four counts and then repeat the stroke. Breathing is easy with the sidestroke since the mouth is out of the water. Breathe in during the power phase of the leading arm and breathe out during the power phase of the trailing arm.

Trudgen

There are several variations of the trudgen, including the trudgen crawl and the double trudgen. Swimmers use the trudgen and its variations, because they take less energy than the front crawl.

Kick. The trudgen uses the scissors kick. Between kicks, the legs rest and trail in the water. The scissors kick usually is shorter in the trudgen than in the sidestroke.

Arm Stroke. The arm strokes are the same as those for the front crawl.

Breathing and Coordination. Coordinate the arm movements and scissors kick as in the sidestroke. If you are doing the trudgen crawl, do two or three flutter kicks between scissors kicks. In the double trudgen, there are two scissors kicks for each arm cycle but no flutter kicks. Roll onto your side to breathe. As the arm on your breathing side completes the power phase and begins the recovery phase, turn on your side and take a breath.

This interesting stroke was named for English swimmer John Trudgen, who introduced the stroke in competition in 1875.

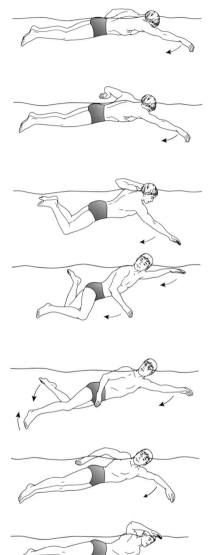

Trudgen, side view

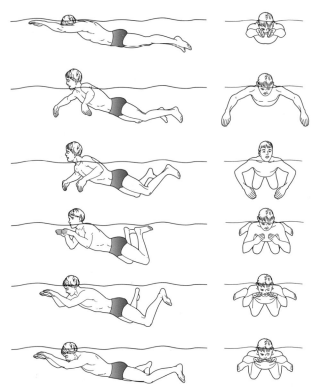

Breaststroke, side and front views

The breaststroke is one of the oldest strokes used in Scouting.

Breaststroke

Variations of the breaststroke range from a restful distance stroke to a competitive racing stroke. With a longer glide as\ taught in Scouting, the breaststroke is a powerful, long-distance stroke that conserves energy and has applications in lifesaving. The stroke uses a whip kick and a shallow arm pull.

Kick. The breaststroke kick, or whip kick, starts in the glide position. Bring your heels toward the hips as far as possible just beneath the water's surface. Keeping your knees bent, spread your knees until they are no farther apart than hip width. Your feet must be farther apart than your knees. Keep your ankles fully flexed and your toes pointed outward. This is the catch position. To begin the power phase, move your feet and lower legs in a whipping motion, pushing outward and backward until your legs and feet are touching in a glide position. At the end of the power phase, your toes should be pointed back and away from your body. As in the scissors kick, the speed of the whip kick should increase rapidly and continue until the end of the kick.

Arm Stroke. Start from a prone float with your arms out straight. Slightly bend your wrists and point your fingers downward. Turn your hands to a slightly palms-out position. Then bend your arms a little at the elbows as the palms and arms push out and down until your hands are farther apart than the width of your shoulders. This is the catch position. Begin the power phase by pressing your arms and palms downward until your elbows form a 90-degree angle, with your forearms pointing toward the bottom. During the power phase, your hands and forearms should always be below the elbows and your elbows should always be below your shoulders. The arm pull should feel as though you are grabbing the water ahead of you and pulling yourself forward until your head passes your hands. Begin the recovery phase by bringing your hands in together under the chin and your elbows to the sides of your body. Finish the recovery by pushing your hands forward just under the surface, fingers leading, until your arms are at their full length in a glide position.

Breathing and Coordination. While doing the breaststroke, you should exhale slowly in the water between breaths. Between the catch and the power phase, lift your chin out of the water, finish exhaling, and quickly take a breath. As your arms begin the recovery phase, place your chin and face back in the water. The water level should be between your eyebrows and hairline. Avoid lifting your head and shoulders too far out of the water to prevent bobbing and losing forward momentum.

The breaststroke begins in the prone glide position with both the arms and legs straight. To coordinate the kick, the arm stokes, and the breathing, think of the phrase, "pull, breathe, kick, glide." As your arms complete the power phase, take a breath, and then draw your feet toward the hips. When your arms are about halfway through the recovery phase, begin the whip kick. Time the arm strokes and kick so that the arms and legs are both at their full length as the kick finishes. Rest in the prone position as your body glides through the water. When the glide begins slow down, it is time to start another stroke.

The pattern the hands trace in the breaststroke is sometimes described as an upside-down heart.

Elementary backstroke, side and top views

Elementary Backstroke

The elementary backstroke is the resting stroke for the last 50 yards of your test. Use this stroke for long-distance swimming or when you are tiring and want to rest while continuing to make forward progress.

Kick. The elementary backstroke uses the whip kick. Floating on your back, spread your knees no farther apart than hip width. Drop your heels by bending your knees. Keep your knees just below the surface. Turn your feet so your toes are pointing out and your ankles are fully flexed up. This is the catch position. To begin the power phase, move your feet and lower legs in a whipping motion to trace an oval shape. Your feet must move outward wider than the position of your knees. End the kick with your legs straight and feet touching. Your toes should be pointed and just below the water's surface. Drop your heels down to begin the recovery phase.

Arm Stroke. The arm stroke for the elementary backstroke is simple. Start on your back in the glide position. Keep your legs straight with your toes pointed and have your arms at your sides with your hands on your thighs. Slowly move your hands either up the centerline of your chest or up the sides of your body with your elbows tucked in until your hands reach the shoulders. Without pausing, straighten out your arms with your palms facing your feet. In a single motion, sweep your arms quickly toward your feet, bending your elbows and wrists throughout the stroke to push water backward. Recover the arms by bringing your hands back up toward your shoulders.

To avoid getting water in your mouth and nose, keep your forehead slightly higher than your chin as your arms push toward your feet.

Breathing and Coordination. In the elementary backstroke, the arms and the legs provide power at the same time. The kick takes less time than the arms because the legs move a shorter distance than the arms, and they are stronger. For these reasons, you should begin the recovery of the arms before the legs. Don't begin the kick until your arms have begun their power phase. With some practice, you should be able to time it so that you finish both the kick and arm stroke together. Strive to make your movements continuous. At the conclusion of the stroke, relax and allow your body to glide through the water for three or four seconds. Don't be in a hurry. Remember, this is a resting stroke. When you finish your glide, repeat the process.

Surface Dives

If you want to swim underwater to retrieve an object or explore the bottom, a surface dive is an easy way of going down. This swimming skill is commonly used in snorkeling and lifesaving. There are two ways to do a surface dive: feetfirst from an upright position or headfirst from a forward swimming position.

Feetfirst Surface Dive

While treading water in an upright position, raise yourself partly out of the water by snapping your legs together in a scissors kick and pressing your hands down on the water. Then let yourself sink. As your face goes under, turn your palms out and press upward with your arms and hands. Doing this will send you down fast. Be sure to keep your hands in the water while pushing up. Keep your feet together and toes pointed to streamline your body. When you near the bottom, change to a swimming position by pulling your knees in until you are tucked. Drop your head and start an underwater breaststroke.

Headfirst Surface Dives

The easiest way to do the headfirst pike surface dive is while moving forward with a breaststroke. As you begin a new arm stroke, keep your legs in the glide position and bend sharply at the waist with your head down so that the upper portion of your body is angled toward the bottom. Then reverse the direction of your arm stroke while lifting your legs out of the water and into the air. When you complete the reverse arm motion and leg lift, you will be in a vertical handstand position with your body straight and your arms straight and pointing toward the bottom. In this streamlined position, the weight of your legs above the water will drive you downward. It all should happen quickly in one smooth motion. Once your feet are underwater, you can begin to swim. If you want to go deeper or faster after you are completely beneath the surface, use the breaststroke, which you also can use to swim along the bottom.

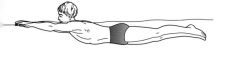

Headfirst surface dive in pike position

A tuck surface dive is another option you can use to fulfill requirement 7b. Instead of lifting your legs as you would for a pike surface dive, pull your knees toward your chest and push them upward as you point your head and arms toward the bottom. The tuck might be a bit easier than the pike to learn at first, but you will not dive as deep or as quickly.

Remember that it is the weight of your legs above you that pushes you down into the water. It is important to get them up into a vertical position in all headfirst surface dives.

Snorkeling and Scuba

Snorkeling, or skin diving, is a sport that a swimmer of any age, size, or strength can enjoy. The sport basically has two activities: (1) the relatively passive activity of floating or swimming on the surface using a breathing tube and eye cover to view underwater scenes, and (2) breath-hold diving to swim and explore underwater environments or recover submerged items.

The Selection and Fit of Equipment

There are four basic pieces of snorkeling equipment: mask, snorkel, fins, and vest.

The Mask

The most important piece of snorkeling equipment is the mask. Because human eyes are designed to see through air, the mask provides the necessary airspace through which the eyes can focus clearly. Additionally, the mask keeps water out of your nose so that you can use the breathing tube more comfortably.

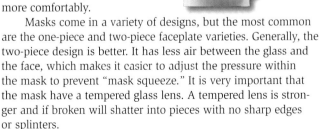

Masks come in a variety of designs, but the most common are the one-piece and two-piece faceplate varieties. Generally, the two-piece design is better. It has less air between the glass and the face, which makes it easier to adjust the pressure within the mask to prevent "mask squeeze." It is very important that the mask have a tempered glass lens. A tempered lens is stronger and if broken will shatter into pieces with no sharp edges or splinters.

Avoid masks made of polyvinyl chloride (PVC) or other plastics.

The part of the mask that fits against the face is called the skirt. Most mask skirts are made of either clear or colored silicone or black neoprene. The neoprene is generally less expensive and is acceptable, but silicone usually lasts longer. Silicone also is a bit softer and more pliable and will more easily fit the contours of the face. A double skirt will provide a better fit for more comfort and less leakage.

Be sure the mask covers the nose but does not cover or interfere with the mouth. The mask should have an exposed nose piece ("nose pocket") or pinch holes for the nose. This allows you to equalize pressure in your ears easily with one hand. Some masks feature a purge valve on the nose pocket or faceplate for clearing water from the mask. However, such valves tend to leak and easily malfunction. They are not needed, because a diver can easily remove water from the mask without these. A good mask also needs a noncorrodible band that holds the lens securely in the skirt and a split, adjustable head strap, which prevents slipping and is much more comfortable.

If the mask has all the features recommended above, then the deciding factor on selection is fit. To check the fit of the mask, place it against your face without using the strap and inhale lightly through your nose (be sure no hair is trapped between skin and skirt). The mask should seal against your face and feel secure with no air leakage. If air leaks into the mask, try other styles and sizes until you have a no-leak fit. If a mask leaks air, it will leak water.

Before putting on the mask, adjust the strap. Undo the strap locks, or "keepers," and move the strap a notch at a time with your finger. Do not grab the loose end or middle of the strap and try to pull it tighter or looser. If the mask fits properly, the strap's only job will be to hold the mask in place. Tightening the strap is not recommended to stop leaks. Doing so will further distort the skirt and cause additional leakage.

To prevent fogging, keep the inside of your lens clean and use a commercial no-fog spray. Other substances, such as saliva, can reduce fogging, but none works as well as the no-fog spray.

With the strap properly adjusted, there are a couple of ways to put on the mask. One way is to put the mask over your face, inhale lightly to hold it, and then use both hands to slip the strap gently over your head and into place. You also may reverse the process by putting the strap in place and then, while holding the strap in place with one hand, pulling the mask forward and down into position over your face. Have your buddy examine the mask to be sure no hair is under the skirt, the straps aren't twisted, and the skirt is properly fitted.

The Snorkel

Snorkels come in many designs, but all feature an oblong, curved rubber mouthpiece with a T-shaped tab molded on each side of the air hole. The longest part of the J-shaped tube is 10 to 14 inches long and may have a slight bend toward the head. The tube should be about ³/₄ inch to 1 inch in diameter. A snorkel should not be more than 14 inches long or less than ³/₄ inch in diameter. You can use your thumb to determine if the snorkel is the proper diameter for you. Insert your thumb into the open end of the snorkel. If your thumb fits, the snorkel is the correct diameter for you. If your thumb is too big to fit inside, choose a snorkel with a larger diameter. The mouthpiece of your snorkel also may contain a purge valve, a one-way valve that allows water to drain out of the snorkel at its lowest point.

Simply slipping the tube under the strap may change the mask fit and put the snorkel at an uncomfortable angle.

There are several ways to attach the snorkel to the mask strap. A snorkel holder, or keeper, usually comes with the snorkel. Two common types of keepers are a rigid tube clip that attaches to the mask strap and a rubber strip that loops around the snorkel tube and under the mask strap. Securing the snorkel to the mask strap prevents loss and adds comfort.

With the snorkel attached to the mask, place the curved flare of the mouthpiece between your lips and gums while you bite gently on the tabs to hold it in place and keep it watertight. While floating or swimming facedown on the surface, breathing through the snorkel's mouthpiece should be easy and natural. When you are ready to dive, inhale deeply and hold your breath until you have completed your dive and have returned to your facedown position at the surface. Of course, the snorkel tube will fill with water during your dive. You cannot resume breathing until it is cleared. This is why you need to hold your breath until your dive is completed. Once your snorkel tube is above the surface, simply exhale sharply to "blast" the water from the tube.

An alternative method for clearing the snorkel is the displacement method. While coming up from your dive, look up so that the snorkel points down. As your face-plate breaks the surface, exhale and roll forward to the facedown position. This should clear the snorkel with a little less effort than the "blast" and avoids the surfacing "blowhole" effect.

Snorkeling Kicks

The kicks used in snorkeling are the flutter kick and the dolphin kick. You may use the flutter kick both on the surface and underwater. The kick should flow

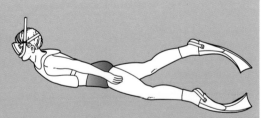

smoothly and slowly from the hips to the toes of the fins. The dolphin kick is useful for short bursts of speed while swimming underwater or coming up from a dive. To do the dolphin kick, hold your legs together and move them in an up-and-down motion with your toes pointed as in the flutter kick. The leg action helps propel you through the water.

The Fins

Swim fins are wedge-shaped, flexible devices worn on the feet to add more power to the kick. When wearing fins while swimming and diving with a snorkel, you usually won't need to do an arm stroke.

When choosing a pair of fins, comfort is very important. Comfort is a function of fit, blade (the paddlelike front of the fin), length, and blade tension. The foot pocket should hold the foot comfortably and snugly. For the beginner or casual snorkeler, a relatively flexible blade of moderate length (24 inches maximum) is recommended.

A full-foot fin has a soft rubber foot pocket. It fits like a shoe over the bare foot. Open-heel adjustable fins also are available, but you may need to buy neoprene boots for a comfortable fit.

The Vest

The vest is a flotation safety device that is not required for snorkeling in confined areas of clear water with a 12-foot maximum depth, such as a swimming pool. However, you should use a properly fitted vest for open-water snorkeling or when snorkeling in water deeper than 12 feet. It should fit over your head and have a back strap or crotch strap to hold it in place. A snorkeling vest also must have a way to add and release air to adjust the buoyancy.

The most common inflation feature is a short tube attached to the upper portion of the vest that you can reach easily with your mouth. A valve in the tube allows you to inflate the vest by blowing into the tube or to deflate it by manually triggering a valve release. Some vests also have a compressed air cartridge for emergency use.

The vest is not simply an emergency device. By partially inflating the vest, you can adjust your floating or swimming position on the surface, gain extra buoyancy, and make swimming easier for longer periods or distances.

It is best to put on the fins while sitting on the dive platform of a boat or at the water's edge, where you can slide into the water without having to stand up or walk. Walking in fins is a good way to fall and hurt yourself.

BSA Snorkeling Safety

BSA Snorkeling Safety is the recommended procedure for conducting BSA swimming activities using masks, fins, and snorkels. Since snorkeling is a swimming activity, Safe Swim Defense guidelines apply. The BSA Snorkeling Safety clarifies and builds upon Safe Swim Defense concepts to situations encountered during training and open-water snorkeling.

1. **Qualified Supervision.** All swimming activity, including snorkeling, must be supervised by a mature and conscientious adult age 21 or older who understands and knowingly accepts responsibility for the well-being and safety of the youth members in his or her care; who is experienced in the water and confident of his or her ability to respond in the event of an emergency; and who is trained in and committed to compliance with the eight points of BSA Safe Swim Defense.

   An experienced snorkeler must supervise snorkeling instruction and open-water snorkeling activities. At a minimum, the supervisor must possess skills and knowledge matching the Snorkeling BSA Award, and have experience with environments similar to those of the planned activity. The supervisor is responsible for compliance with each point of BSA Snorkeling Safety.

   Unit leaders may rely on the expertise of other adults to supplement their knowledge and training. They may delegate the task of supervision, for example, when the unit is participating in a snorkeling activity conducted by a tour operator, provided they are satisfied that the operator's training and experience will provide a safe activity with appropriate safeguards.

2. **Physical Health Review.** A complete health history from physician, parent, or legal guardian is required of all participants as evidence of fitness for snorkeling activities. Participants should be asked to relate any recent incidents of illness or injury just prior to the activity. Supervision and protection should be adjusted

to anticipate any potential risks associated with individual health conditions. Recent sinus or ear infections may temporarily preclude surface dives while snorkeling. Those with known adverse reactions to stings from marine life, or with chronic conditions such as diabetes or asthma, may need special medications at hand. Adults with known risk factors for cardiovascular disease should not undertake strenuous activities without the advice of their physician. In the event of any significant health conditions, a medical evaluation by a physician should be required by the adult leader.

3. **Safe Area**. Training in the use of snorkeling equipment shall be performed in clear water in a confined area that conforms to Safe Swim Defense guidelines. "Clear water" implies pool-like visibility. At a minimum, an 8-inch disk with white and black quadrants at a depth of 8 feet should be recognizable from above the surface. "Confined area" denotes either a pool or an established summer camp swimming area with direct access from the shore or a dock.

   Safe conditions for open-water swimming and snorkeling depend on water clarity, area definition, depth, access, and other environmental factors. Snorkeling is limited to clear water. "Open water" denotes a temporary swimming area of flexible extent in a natural body of water that may not be close to shore.

   An open-water snorkeling area need not have physical boundary markers, but the activity should be restricted within a specified distance of a point on shore, an anchored vessel, a moving rescue craft, or a float with a dive flag attached. Generally, a 50-foot radius is recommended, and may be dictated by local regulations concerning the use of a dive flag. The area covered by the snorkeling group should be small enough to allow rapid assistance from rescue personnel.

   Emergency response places limitations on safe water depth as well as water clarity and area. Response personnel should be able to quickly and easily reach the bottom, and locate, recover, and transport a submerged victim to shore or vessel. At the start of the activity, and periodically if the group moves along a reef or other feature, the response personnel should check their ability both to see and to reach the bottom. The group should be directed toward shallower water whenever the responders experience any difficulty. (Twelve feet is designated as a reasonable maximum depth in Safe Swim Defense. In practice, slightly shallower or deeper depths may be appropriate. Different personnel will be able to easily recover objects from different depths, particularly if wearing fins. The practical way to confirm a safe depth is to test that the bottom is within comfortable reach of all designated rescue personnel.)

Limited or distant access to the snorkeling area may require additional consideration. Underwater features close to a sloping beach or near an anchored vessel are ideal. If the snorkeling site is a considerable distance from a beach or permitted anchoring location, the ability to rest becomes important and may restrict the activity close to shallow water or dictate the use of inflatable vests and/or small response craft. Tide tables should be consulted in areas with large tidal changes, especially when beach access is at the base of a cliff. Snorkeling in a river may require an exit point downstream of the entry.

Snorkeling should not be done if water depth, clarity, or temperature, boat traffic, waves, current, weather, marine life, or bottom conditions, including vegetation, are deemed unsafe by the qualified supervisor. Time in the water should be adjusted based on water temperature and sun exposure. Snorkeling at night is limited to lighted pools unless the activity is conducted at a BSA nationally accredited high-adventure base.

4. Proper Equipment

a. All snorkeling equipment shall be properly fitted and in good repair.

b. The use of inflatable snorkeling vests and personal flotation devices is at the discretion of the qualified supervisor based on local conditions and the abilities of the participants and responders. Use of individual flotation devices is required in open water whenever there is a noticeable current or swells, when the bottom is not visible from the surface (due to vegetation or limited visibility beyond 8 feet), or when the activity is an extended distance (more than 50 yards) from shore or craft.

c. A dive flag should be used at all open water sites. It may be displayed from a dive boat or attached to a float and towed with the snorkeling party. Local rules and regulations may specify the type of flag and how close snorkelers must stay to it.

d. Protective clothing may be worn. Gloves are appropriate in areas with sharp rocks or encrusted structures. A shirt or a diver's body suit will provide limited protection from sun, abrasion, or coral burns and minor insulation in warm water. In temperate water, a partial or full wet suit may be worn. Weight belts may not be used.

e. Lifesaving equipment in good repair shall be ready for immediate use by response personnel. A flotation device is recommended, such as a rescue tube, bodyboard, or PFD, supplemented, as appropriate, by reaching and throwing devices, and small craft. Dive boats should be equipped with radios and first-aid kits, and should deploy a safety line.

5. Response Personnel.
It is the responsibility of the qualified supervisor to designate personnel for emergency response whenever lifeguards are not provided by a facility or tour operator. The snorkeling party should be divided into groups of two to eight swimmers with two responders, paired as buddies, assigned to each group.

(Units may be divided by patrols or crews.) The responders should be competent swimmers with basic water rescue skills. Emergency procedures, including entries, exits, and the role of everyone in the group, should be reviewed and practiced prior to the activity using rescue aids at the site.

The responders should be stationed either afloat or ashore where they can see and hear all those in their group. Neither the responders nor the swimmers should face into the sun to see the other. Snorkelers in a group should remain off the same side of a vessel. Inflatable or rigid dinghies with oars are appropriate response craft. The responders and snorkelers should remain close enough for rapid rescue, generally within 50 feet of one another. In some situations, the qualified supervisor may deem it appropriate for the responders to tow rescue aids while accompanying their group in the water.

Responders are responsible for surveillance as well as rescue. If there is more than one group, then a separate lookout, who may be the qualified supervisor, should coordinate the entire activity and monitor changing conditions. The lookout should have audible or visible means, such as an air horn or flag, to recall all groups. If a boat is used to transport snorkelers to the site, then at least one person should remain aboard who knows how to drive the boat and use the radio. A least one person in the party must be trained in CPR.

It is the combined responsibility of the adult supervisor, the lookout, and the responders to know the number of people in the water at all times and to make frequent visible confirmations of that number. Buddy boards and tags, or their equivalent, must be used to account for everyone in the water.

6. **Ability.** Only those who have completed the Snorkeling BSA requirements may participate in open-water snorkeling. Scouts classified as beginners or nonswimmers

may use snorkeling equipment in clear, confined water of appropriate depth, as specified in Safe Swim Defense (points 3 and 6), during instructional swims or during closely supervised recreational activity. Training for the Snorkeling BSA Award is limited to Scouts and adults classified as swimmers.

7. **Buddy System.** All participants in snorkeling activities are paired as buddies. Buddies should check each other's equipment prior to the activity and review hand signals. During the activity, they should remain close enough that they are constantly aware of their buddy's location and condition. Generally, buddies should take turns making breath-holding dives. That is, one buddy remains at the surface, floating with his mask in the water while breathing through the snorkel, and keeps an eye on the buddy who is down. When the diver surfaces, both buddies check their position relative to the group before moving on or letting the other buddy dive.

The adult supervisor, lookout, or responders may call buddy checks as needed to keep the buddies together. Buddy checks may also be called to aid communication. Buddy pairs should be instructed to routinely watch for predetermined audible and visual signals of a buddy check.

8. **Discipline.** Be sure everyone understands and agrees that snorkeling is allowed only with proper supervision and use of the complete Safe Swim Defense and BSA Snorkeling Safety standards. The applicable rules should be presented and learned prior to the outing, and should be reviewed for all participants at the beginning of the snorkeling activity. Scouts should respect and follow all directions and rules of the adult supervisor. When people know the reason for rules and procedures they are more likely to follow them. Treatment should be strict and fair, without favoritism.

Earn the Snorkeling BSA swimsuit patch by completing the requirements found in your *Boy Scout Requirements* book (current year) or the Snorkeling BSA application, No. 19-176.

Search and Recovery

When you surface from a dive, have one hand over your head to protect yourself from objects on the surface.

A team of snorkelers can systematically search an area by slowly moving forward, side by side on the surface, while looking at the bottom. When one snorkeler sees the search object or an area that needs closer inspection, that snorkeler dives while the others stay at their surface position so the diver can return to the search line. A single snorkeler should search across the area and then return on a close parallel course, continuing back and forth until the entire search area has been covered.

If a search area has been covered by a search team or individual without recovery, it should be covered again with a line of search at a right angle to the first search. If the grid-pattern search is unsuccessful, an alternative search-and-recovery method should be considered.

Scuba in Scouting

Swimming underwater using a Self-Contained Underwater Breathing Apparatus (scuba) can be great fun, but it also can be dangerous and even fatal. However, when proper safety precautions are taken, scuba diving as a sport has an excellent safety record. This record comes mainly from the quality training programs developed by the scuba-diving industry. Scouting relies on such training to provide safe scuba opportunities for its members.

Introductory Scuba

There are several levels of scuba training. Basic introductory experiences are conducted in pools with a small group supervised by a certified instructor. If you complete one of these courses, you will get a taste of the sport under controlled conditions, although such a course will not prepare or certify you to dive on your own. Scuba BSA for qualified Scouts, Scouters, and Venturers is one of those programs. Requirements are found in the Scuba BSA brochure, No. 19-515. Slightly more advanced introductory courses conclude with an open-water dive under close supervision. Open-water dives are not an option for Scuba BSA.

Open-Water Certification

Open-water certification courses provide the training needed for independent diving with a buddy and are normally required before a person is allowed to fill or rent tanks. Numerous tour operators and dive shops arrange group dive trips for people so certified. Standard open-water certification is offered only to those over a certain age. Junior diver certification is available for those below that age. Scouts and Venturers age 14 or older are approved to enroll in either standard or junior certification programs as a Scouting activity.

After obtaining open-water certification a diver may pursue a number of underwater activities including underwater photography, wreck diving, cave diving, cold-water diving, and diver rescue. Divers with a sufficient number of logged dives and additional training may qualify for a divemaster rating. Divemaster is the minimum qualification needed by the dive supervisor when certified divers engage in unit dives during Scouting activities.

All scuba instruction must be conducted by certified scuba instructors. Units that are interested in scuba training can find Scout camps that offer training programs under the high-adventure listing on the BSA Web site *(http://www.scouting.org)*. The National High Adventure Florida Sea Base *(http://www.seabase.org)* offers scuba training and dive programs. Training also may be arranged through the agencies identified in the BSA Scuba Policy.

Get your parent's permission before exploring scuba online.

BSA Scuba Policy

Any person possessing, displaying, or using scuba (self-contained underwater breathing apparatus) in connection with any Scouting-related activity must either be currently certified by, or enrolled in, a training course authorized by the National Association of Underwater Instructors (NAUI), the Professional Association of Diving Instructors (PADI), or Scuba Schools International (SSI). These agencies are recognized by the Boy Scouts of America for scuba training and instruction. Alternatively, if PADI, NAUI, or SSI training and instruction is not available, certification may be accepted from other agencies that comply with Recreational Scuba Training Council (RSTC) guidelines, provided that such acceptance has been expressly approved by the BSA local council in consultation with the national BSA Health and Safety Service.

Cub Scouts. Youth members in Cub Scouting are not authorized to use scuba in any activity.

Boy Scouts and Varsity Scouts. The use of scuba is not authorized for a BSA unit, except that registered Boy Scout youth and leaders may participate in the Scuba BSA program conducted by a certified dive instructor in compliance with this policy. Scuba BSA is not a diver certification program.

Scuba training programs may be a part of troop/team activities for participants who are 14 years of age or older. Members who meet the age requirement and are properly certified may participate in group dives under the supervision of a responsible adult who is currently certified as a dive master, assistant instructor, or any higher rating from NAUI, PADI, or SSI. Student divers must be under the supervision of a currently certified NAUI, PADI, or SSI instructor. (Leaders trained by other RSTC agencies may be utilized with local council and National Council approval.) No exceptions to the BSA age requirement are permitted. Scouts with a junior diver certification may dive only when accompanied by a buddy who is a certified open-water diver at least 18 years old.

Venturers. Scuba programs may be a part of Venturing activities for participants who are 14 years of age or older. Members who meet the age requirement and are properly certified may participate in group dives under the supervision of a responsible adult who is currently certified as a dive master, assistant instructor, or any higher rating from NAUI, PADI, or SSI. Student divers must be under the supervision of a currently certified NAUI, PADI, or SSI instructor. No exceptions to the BSA age requirement are permitted.

Diving

Diving is fun. Springboard diving is a good muscle builder and teaches you to make your whole body work gracefully. Before you try board diving, you will need to have mastered elementary diving skills. And remember, always check the water before any dive to make sure it is deep enough and there is nothing in the way.

Elementary Diving

The steps in learning elementary diving are the kneeling start, the bent-knee start, and the standing dive.

Kneeling Start. Kneel on one knee and hook the toes of your other foot over the edge of the pool. Bend forward with your chin down toward your chest. Keeping your arms straight, place them against your ears with your hands together. Lean forward and slide into the water, always leading with your hands and the top of your head. Push with your foot against the edge of the pool. Straighten your body and legs and bring your feet together as you go into the water. To return to the surface, point your hands up and your body will follow.

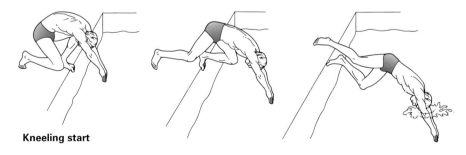

Kneeling start

After you have practiced the kneeling start a few times, raise up from the kneeling position so that both knees are off the deck. Keeping the formerly bent knee behind the edge of the pool and the other foot near the edge, assume a running position. With your arms and head in the same position as for the kneeling start, bend toward the water. As you begin to fall forward, push off toward the water. Bring your feet together as you enter the water.

Bent-Knee Start. Stand with your knees slightly bent and your feet about 5 to 10 inches apart. Your toes should be gripping the edge. Bend forward at the waist with your chin toward your chest. Keep your arms straight and placed against your ears. Fall forward and enter the water 3 to 4 feet from the side. As you fall forward, keep your chin down and push up with your feet.

Bent-knee start

Standing Dive. Stand with your legs straight and your feet together. Bend forward with your chin toward your chest. Keep your arms straight and place them against your ears. Fall forward and push upward to lift your hips and give height to your dive. Be sure to keep your head down until after you have entered the water. Straighten your legs and keep them together until you are beneath the surface. Practice to improve your form.

Standing dive

Long Shallow Dive

The long shallow dive is performed with your body in a streamlined, arrowlike position that allows you to enter the water with great forward speed at a shallow angle. The dive is usually performed from a standing position. It can be used for fun and for informal racing starts. As in all diving, remember that the water should be clear, of proper depth, and free of dangerous obstacles.

Once you have learned the standing dive, it is easy to learn the long shallow dive. Start with your feet in a comfortable position on the edge of the deck. They should be 6 to 8 inches apart with your toes gripping the edge. Your knees and hips should be flexed and your back almost parallel to the deck. Let your arms hang down in a relaxed, loose fashion with your head up and eyes focused on a point in the water about two body lengths from the edge. Start the forward motion by swinging your arms backward and up toward your hips. Allow your heels to rise and your body to lean forward. Then immediately swing your arms down and forward, and straighten your legs with a powerful thrust. Doing this will drive your body out over the water in a position almost parallel to the surface.

During this flight, drop your head slightly to a point between your outstretched arms, which should be angled slightly toward the water. You should enter the water at a slight angle. Do not allow your body to land flat on the water. It will slow you down, and you could hurt yourself. Keep your arms straight and your toes pointed, with your body in an arrowlike position during the underwater glide. As the glide slows, start kicking. This will bring you to the surface, where you can begin a swimming stroke.

The long shallow dive is a recreational dive that also can be used for lifesaving approaches and when you are racing for fun. When you have learned this dive, you might be ready to be coached for a racing dive. Racing dives should only be taught by and practiced in the presence of an experienced swimming coach. Never dive from racing start blocks unless you have been properly trained and are supervised.

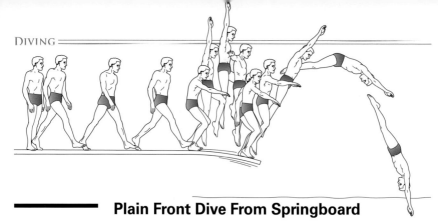

Plain Front Dive From Springboard

If you have never been on a board before, your instructor may have you first practice with a simple feetfirst entry.

Springboard diving involves a proper starting position and approach to the end of the board, a hurdle or jump, a takeoff from the board, flight in the air, and the entry. Practice diving from a board about 3 feet or 1 meter above the water. First, get used to the extra height above the water by practicing a simple standing dive from the end of the board the same way you did at the edge of the pool.

The next step is to learn the approach and hurdle. Most divers use three steps before the hurdle. Your instructor may have you first learn the approach on dry land before moving to the board. Practice on land with a line to represent the end of the board. This exercise also will allow you to judge how far from the end of the board you should start.

Take the first step with your jumping leg—the leg that gives you the most power when you jump from it. Keep your head up and focus your eyes on the line on the deck or the end of the board. Your second step follows your first. Let your arms swing naturally at your sides as if you were walking down the street. Take the third step with your jumping leg. This step should be about a foot longer than the first two. The lengthened stride will help change your forward motion into upward motion.

As your weight moves over your jumping leg, start your hurdle. Swing your arms forward, lifting the opposite knee at the same time. Then drive up from the board with your jumping leg. Bring both arms over your head, keeping the toes of both feet pointing down. When you reach the peak of your hurdle, move your arms out to the side and straighten both legs together with your toes pointed as you drop to the end of the board. Let your toes hit just before your heels so you will land softly. Allow your arms to sweep down slightly behind you, pass next to your hips, and start forward. At the same time, bend your knees a little and lift your head until you are looking across the pool.

As the board starts to spring up, push high into your dive and lift your arms over your head. Use your whole body to dive over an imaginary crossbar located at eye level about a foot in front of the board. Clasp your hands and duck your head, ready for the entry. Aim straight for the bottom, with legs together and toes pointed until you are entirely beneath the surface.

Diving Safety

Scouting has specific guidelines for safe diving and elevated water entry. "Diving" refers to any water entry in which the feet do not make first contact with the water. "Elevated entry" refers to any water entry from a height more than 18 inches above the water. BSA Safe Swim Defense guidelines do not permit diving or swimming activity of any kind in water deeper than 12 feet. No elevated entry is permitted where the person must clear any obstacle, including jumping or diving over land.

In water with less than 7 feet of unobstructed depth, diving is not permitted and water entry must be feetfirst. A leaping entry is recommended where water is at or above head level. A step-down or jump-down entry from a sitting position is recommended for shallower water. Never attempt to plunge headfirst below waves at a beach.

Diving is permitted in clear water more than 7 feet deep from a dock, pier, or platform that is no more than 18 inches above the water surface. For elevated diving from a height between 18 and 40 inches, the water must be unobstructed and at least 10 feet deep. The water must be clear enough to enable supervisory and lifeguard personnel to see the diver at the deepest part of the plunge.

Board diving is permitted only from boards that are mounted on a fixed (not floating) platform or deck, no more than 40 inches (approximately 1 meter) above the water surface. Clear water depth below the board should be 10 to 12 feet. A lifeguard or supervisor should be positioned where the diver can be seen at all times beneath the surface. There should be no other surface or underwater activity or obstruction for at least 15 feet on either side of the board and 25 feet in front of the board.

Any elevated entry from a height greater than 40 inches must be feetfirst and only from a fixed platform or solid footing no higher than the person is tall. Clear water depth should be 10 to 12 feet. Other protective measures and distances are the same as for board diving.

Diving always should be done straight ahead from the board, never to the sides.

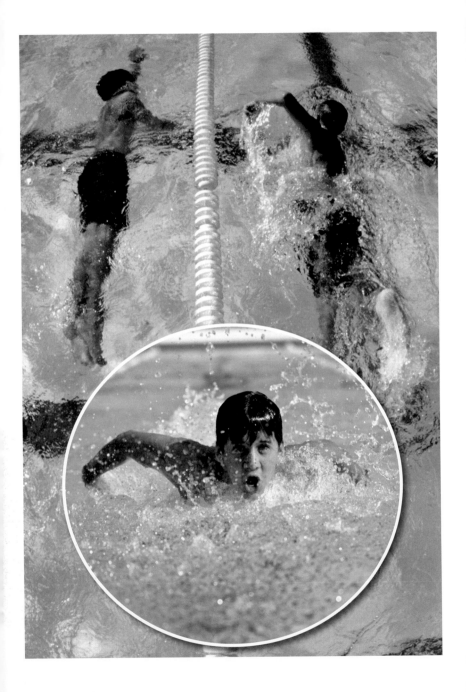

Competitive Swimming

The swimming strokes you have learned in Scouting stress energy conservation, safety, and function rather than speed. In competitive swimming, however, speed is key. To swim at a competitive level, improve your physical conditioning and play close attention to skills.

Competitive Strokes

To complete requirement 8b, you must demonstrate good form on one competitive swimming stroke. If you select the front crawl, back crawl, or breaststroke, you already have a strong basic stroke foundation and will need to make only a few changes for racing form. If you enjoy the challenge of learning a new stroke, you can master the unique butterfly stroke, which is used mainly for competition and vigorous exercise.

During very short races, such as a 50-meter race, freestyle swimmers might take only three breaths during the entire race.

Front Crawl or Trudgen

There are only a few differences between the front crawl stroke and competitive crawl, or "freestyle," stroke. Depending on the length of the race, a competitive freestyle swimmer may use different beats for the flutter kick. For short races, sprinters prefer the six-beat kick. However, for long distances you may find that a two-beat kick or the trudgen scissors kick is more energy-efficient. You also can change the breathing rhythm so that instead of breathing every one, two, three, or more strokes on the same side, you breathe on one side and then the other. This alternating breathing style allows for a breath once every one-and-a-half arm cycles.

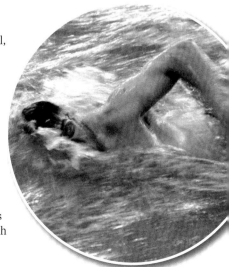

Backstroke (Back Crawl)

In backstroke competition, swimmers push off on their backs and continue swimming on their backs throughout the race. The form for the racing backstroke is the same as for the form used when not in competition. However, the start requires the use of a starting block so that you can lift yourself out of the water while leaving your toes underwater.

Opportunities for a Career in Swimming

People who enjoy swimming-related activities and who have a passion for swimming might be surprised at the career opportunities this sport has to offer. In addition to coaching (swimming, diving, water polo, and so on) and private instruction at the recreational, amateur, and professional levels, there are opportunities as swim trainers; water aerobics instructors; in management as aquatics directors and coordinators; in sports science, and in many other aquatics-related fields. You might begin to explore the possibilities through your merit badge counselor or career counselor at school.

Breaststroke

To change the basic breaststroke from an easy, restful, distance-swimming stroke to a high energy racing stroke, you leave out the long glide and shorten the recovery phase. Leaving out the long glide allows the stroke to be swum continuously. The increase in the number of strokes per minute and the shortened recovery phase make the racing breaststroke much more physically demanding than the basic stroke. At the beginning of the recovery phase (when your hands are under your chin), shoot them forward with great force and out over the water. Dive your head under the water (to reduce drag and resistance) as your arms reach forward and your legs do a whip kick.

Butterfly stroke, side and front views

Butterfly

The butterfly is the second fastest of the competitive strokes and is used only in racing and for high-energy exercise. The stroke is so named because both arms recover at the same time and give the appearance of a butterfly winging through the air. The stroke also is unique because it is the only stroke to use the dolphin kick, a kick that looks like the powerful motion of a dolphin's tail.

Kick. For the dolphin kick, you hold your legs together and move both of them in an up-and-down motion at the same time. Start by straightening your legs and bringing them together with the toes pointed as in the flutter kick. Bend your knees as you bring your feet forward and upward and drop the hips slightly in the water. When your lower leg is at a 45-degree angle with your body, begin the downbeat of the kick. Straighten your legs as you would for the downbeat of the flutter kick. As your legs kick down, your hips will lift. Your heels and feet should just break the water's surface.

Arm Stroke. During the arm stroke of the butterfly, both arms move together at the same time. Begin the arm pull with your arms straightened and in front of your body and your palms facing outward. Your arms should be about shoulder width apart. This is the catch position. Start the power phase by turning your palms inward as your hands press downward. Bend your elbows with the downward hand motion and bend the neck back, bringing your head upward. Continue bending your elbows as you bring your hands inward toward your body. As your arms reach a 90-degree angle to your body, raise your head out of the water. Your hands will be halfway through the pull.

The path that the arms follow in the butterfly stroke is called a keyhole or hourglass pattern.

Allow your hands to continue their path backward as you straighten your elbows. Continue until your arms are fully straightened and your hands are alongside your upper legs. For the recovery phase, bring your arms back to the front of your body in a semicircular arc just above the water's surface. Your hands, with the palms outward, will enter the water as you straighten your elbows to return to the starting position.

Breathing and Coordination. In the butterfly stroke, you perform two dolphin kicks with each arm-pull cycle. Begin the first kick by lowering your hips and starting the downbeat of the legs as your hands and arms enter the water. Begin the second kick at the halfway point of the arm-pull cycle. As your hands push toward your feet, start the downbeat of the second kick and finish as you lift your arms out of the water for the recovery.

Your body remains flat and facedown in the water, with your hips staying within a few inches of the water's surface. As you move forward, keep your head in alignment with your body and your face in the water with your chin tucked against your chest. Slowly exhale underwater during the stroke so that you can quickly inhale when your head naturally rises during the first half of the power phase. Inhale by raising your chin out of the water. Do not lift your shoulders or arch your back to raise your head. Keep your head elevated just until your mouth clears the water, but always keep the lower half of your chin in the water. Take a breath while your arms are in the rear position. As soon as you inhale, return your head to the water.

Typically, a swimmer takes a breath every other stroke because breathing every stroke often slows down the stroke. Some swimmers use the "two up, one down" method of breathing. To try out this method, take a breath for two successive strokes and then keep your head in the water on the next stroke. Swimmers with good lung capacity sometimes use a variation of this method during sprints or toward the finish of a race in which they breathe every third stroke. World-class swimmers breathe so effortlessly that there is no real difference in their speed between when they take a breath and when they don't.

The Racing Dive

The racing start for freestyle, breaststroke, and butterfly must be a dive from a standing position. Several techniques are used in competitive swimming. For the racing start known as the "grab start," you grasp the front edge of the pool or starting block. In this position, your center of gravity is as far forward as possible. This shortens the time required for your body to move forward from a stationary position to a position of forward motion. The arms provide stability and help you keep your balance.

After entering the water, a brief gliding phase follows. In freestyle and butterfly, you are allowed to do an underwater flutter kick or butterfly kick. After swimming no more than 15 meters underwater, you must surface and begin the arm stroke. In the breaststroke, you can take one stroke underwater and allow both arms to pull down all the way to the legs. You also are permitted to do a single downward dolphin kick followed by a breaststroke kick before your head must surface and you begin the breaststroke.

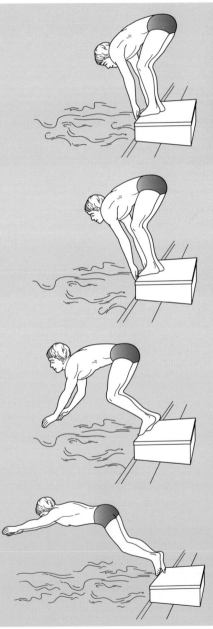

On the signal to take your mark, bend over and grasp the edge of the deck with your toes and with your fingers on either side of your feet. Bend your knees slightly to set your hips high with your weight directly over the balls of your feet. Hang your head comfortably between your shoulders and look at your toes. Straighten up slightly until your arms lock.

On the "go" signal, bring your head up sharply forward to begin the short upward arc of your dive.

Quickly bring your hands forward, keeping them below shoulder level and reaching forward until your arms are at their full length. Push off with your legs and feet.

As quickly as possible, your head and hands reach the highest point and you begin to drive yourself out over the water with a powerful leg push.

As your feet leave the deck, keep the angle of your body nearly horizontal to the water by keeping the hips in a high position.

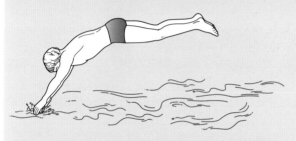

Raise your legs up before your entry into the water. Drop your head down between your arms so your ears are squeezed between your upper arms. Keep your legs and feet together.

Slice cleanly into the water with your hands. The rest of your body should slip through the "hole" opened by your hands. Keep your head tucked low to avoid slapping your face on the water. Even the feet should slip through the "hole" without a splash. Glide just below the surface until you slow to swimming speed, and then begin your stroke.

Racing Turns

Competitive swimming events frequently involve two or more
laps, or pool lengths, so turns are an important racing skill.
Indeed, learning and practicing quick racing turns can be as
important to winning as mastering stroke skills. Turning methods
vary depending on the stroke. Most competitive swimming pools
have bottom and overhead markings, or turn targets, that let you
know when to begin your turn. However, these are not helpful if
you are not watching for them! Always practice swimming in
clear water and with your eyes open. A comfortable, well-fitted
pair of swim goggles is recommended for serious competitors.

Front or Crawl Stroke Flip Turn

The crawl stroke flip turn also is referred to as the tumble turn.

The preparation for this flip turn begins when you are about one
stroke away from the side of the pool. When you reach this
point, do not recover your arm from the last stroke but let it trail
at your side. Take one more stroke and leave that arm trailing at
your side when the stroke is finished. Both palms will be facing
down alongside your legs. Bend at the waist and tuck your chin
to your chest. Tuck up your legs and, leading with your head,
do a half somersault while pulling your palms toward your face.

Be sure to exhale air through your nose throughout the flip
turn to avoid getting water in your nose. You will flip over on
your back underwater (slightly on one side) with your feet against
the wall. Your toes will be pointing up or to the side. Your hands
should be above your head. Push off with your feet from the wall.
As you leave the wall, roll to a prone position, reach forward with
both arms, and glide underwater. As you surface and your glide
slows to swimming speed, begin stroking. Do not take a breath
until the second or third arm stroke.

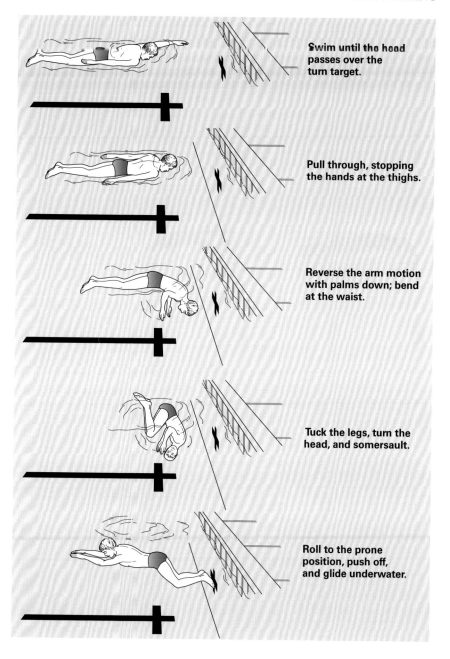

Swim until the head passes over the turn target.

Pull through, stopping the hands at the thighs.

Reverse the arm motion with palms down; bend at the waist.

Tuck the legs, turn the head, and somersault.

Roll to the prone position, push off, and glide underwater.

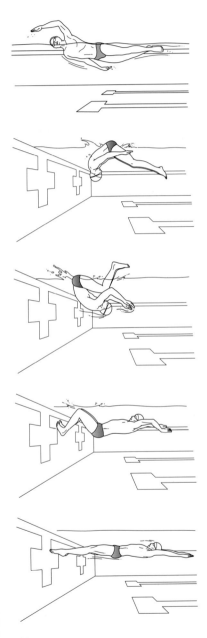

Backstroke Flip Turn

The backstroke flip turn is now used for all serious competition. Since swimmers cannot see the wall behind them while doing the backstroke, competitive pools have flags hanging 5 yards from the end of the pool to warn the backstrokers. Practice first to figure out how many strokes it takes you to swim from the flags to the wall.

Start the flip one stroke from the wall by turning your head and looking toward your pulling arm as it does the catch. As you pull, rotate onto your stomach, drive your head downward, and stop your pulling hand at your hips. At the same time, your other arm recovers across your body, enters the water in the same position as in the front crawl, and then pulls to the hips.

Start the somersault while tucking your knees tightly to your chest. Turn both palms toward your body and sweep them toward your head to complete the flip. Exhale air through your nose throughout the flip turn to avoid getting water in your nose. Keep your legs tucked until your feet contact the wall, toes pointed upward. If you have done the flip correctly, you will be on your back. Push off forcefully and get into a streamlined position as you leave the wall. After you are clear of the wall but still underwater, do several quick dolphin kicks. You are permitted to go as far as 15 meters before having to surface and take a stroke.

Breaststroke and Butterfly Turns

When your head passes the turn target (about 5 feet out), complete the stroke in progress and glide with your arms outstretched until both hands touch the wall. If the pool edge provides a handhold, grab it and pull into the wall. Pull in quickly, tucking your knees tightly under you as you switch directions and turn sideways.

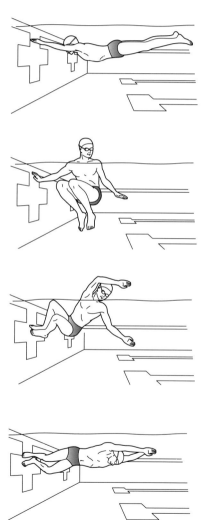

If the wall has no handhold, tuck your legs under you and switch directions while turning sideways. Your knees will remain in a tucked-up position as you plant your feet on the wall. As your feet come under you toward the wall, your head will lift out of the water. Take a quick breath before your head goes back in the water.

As you turn sideways, your top arm will be pointing away from the wall. You may bring this arm in close to the body as you reverse directions by bending the elbow and bringing in the hand or you may leave it out in front. When your feet are moving under your body and your head is switching directions, bring your hand and arm away from the wall, out of the water, and over the top of your head. Submerge yourself and push off the wall with your hands and arms out in front of you. As you leave the wall on your side, turn to a face-down position.

If you are doing the breaststroke, you can take one stroke underwater after pushing off the wall, using both arms to pull down all the way to the legs. You also are permitted to do a single downward dolphin kick followed by a breaststroke kick before your head must break the surface and you begin the arm stroke. If you are doing the butterfly, you are allowed to do dolphin kicks for a maximum of 15 meters underwater. Then you must surface and begin the arm stroke.

Crawl Stroke Open Turn

The crawl stroke open turn is useful for swimming laps or for competitive swimmers who have not yet learned a flip turn. It is very similar to the turn for the breaststroke and butterfly. However, it is not used in serious competition.

When about 5 feet from the wall, or when positioned over a turn target, pull through to the end of an arm stroke, roll onto your side, and glide with your lower arm fully straightened. As your forward hand touches the wall, absorb the momentum by placing the palm flat against the wall. Allow your elbow to bend, keeping your forearm between your head and the wall. As the elbow bends, remain on your side and tuck both knees up to your chin.

If the pool edge provides a handhold, grab it and pull into the wall. Tuck your knees tightly under you as you reverse directions while still on your side. As your feet come under you toward the wall, your head will lift out of the water. Take a quick breath before your head goes back in the water. As you glide into the wall, your top arm will be pointing away from the wall. When you turn to reverse direction, you can tuck the top arm close to the body by bending the elbow and bringing in the hand or you can leave it out in front of you. As your feet move to make contact with the wall and your head and upper body move away from the wall, bring the arm on the wall out of the water and over the top of your head. Submerge yourself and push off the wall with both feet and the hands and arms extended out in front of you. Turn to a facedown position and move into a shallow underwater prone glide. Glide until your speed slows to swimming speed, then begin stroking.

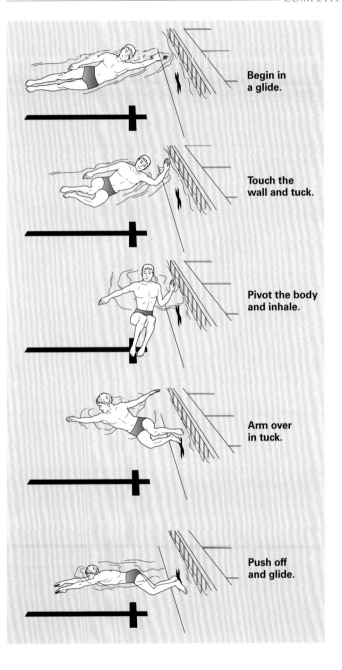

Begin in
a glide.

Touch the
wall and tuck.

Pivot the body
and inhale.

Arm over
in tuck.

Push off
and glide.

Swimming for Fitness and Health

Regular exercise may be the single most important thing a person can do to live a long and healthy life. Studies of people who live to great ages—into their 90s and beyond—indicate that these people have at least one thing in common: regular, consistent exercise. While exercise has a wide variety of benefits, the most remarkable are the prevention of heart disease and the strengthening of bones.

Exercise and Health

The relationship between exercise and heart disease has been investigated extensively. The results are always the same: the physically active have less heart disease. The impact of exercise on heart disease is, in part, due to its beneficial effects on the other risk factors of heart disease.

People who exercise regularly are much less likely to be overweight because exercise burns calories. Exercise reduces blood pressure, too. In fact, the combination of exercise and losing weight often allows people with hypertension (high blood pressure) to control it without taking medicines. This control may be better than was possible with medicines. Research has shown that active male joggers have lower total cholesterol than men of the same age who don't run. There is no substitute for exercise when it comes to protecting your heart.

Without enough exercise, bones become demineralized. That is, they lose their calcium and become brittle. If a person is put to complete bed rest, this process starts almost immediately and progresses rapidly. This is one reason why doctors recommend that people who have had a major operation or a heart attack resume activity as soon as possible.

The demineralization of bones has been documented in astronauts returning from space, where lack of gravity robs physical activity of its exercise value. Weak and brittle bones—a result of a lack of exercise—are also common in the aged.

Exercise is an excellent cardiovascular conditioner and is important to living better as well as longer. People who exercise regularly feel and look younger than those who do not. Improvements in muscle tone and circulation undoubtedly help physically fit people feel more energetic and give them a feeling of well-being. Moreover, research shows that healthy people are more productive at work.

If the importance of exercise is so well-known and obvious, then why do people often neglect to exercise and protect their health? The main reason is choice! Remember your Scout training and Scout Oath—what will be your choice?

Making Exercise Part of Your Life

How, when, and where you choose to exercise will depend on such things as where you live; what facilities and equipment are available to you; and your health, physical abilities, and training. But these things should determine only the type, place, and timing of your exercise, not your basic decision to exercise. Some people may go rock climbing. Others may take daily walks. For some people the choices are almost limitless. For others the choices may be fewer, but everyone can choose to exercise and can gain from doing it.

For those who are limited by choice or circumstances to one form of exercise, a full-body exercise is strongly recommended. In full-body exercise, all the muscles and joints are moved and flexed. Examples of full-body exercise include brisk walking, running, cycling, rowing, and swimming.

Swimming for Exercise

In many respects, swimming is superior to other forms of exercise because it involves all the muscles and joints, is highly aerobic, and has a very low injury rate. In addition, swimming promotes coordination, and the buoyancy effect of water limits stress to the joints. You can improve upper body strength by working on overarm strokes, and focus on leg development with kick drills and swim sprints using the flutter kick. It's not surprising that swimming is often prescribed and used as physical therapy for paralysis, stroke, and injury victims. A regular swimming exercise program will help you increase stamina, polish your swimming skills, and develop an exercise program that you can keep using as you grow older.

Planning a Swimming Exercise Program

Why not enjoy your favorite activity—swimming—and get that ever-so-important exercise at the same time? Simply plan and follow a regular swimming routine, and you've got it.

The five parts of a fitness exercise routine are warm-up, aerobic activity, strength building, flexibility maintenance, and cool-down. You could warm up with a slow-paced 50-yard swim using the sidestroke or breaststroke. A great aerobic workout would be three or four 25-yard swim sprints using an aggressive butterfly or crawl stroke with a one- or two-minute rest between sprints. Follow the sprints with a 300- to 500-yard swim using a crawl or trudgen for a good strength workout. To increase and maintain the flexibility needed for almost every swimming activity, add a few stretching/flexibility exercises to your warm-up and cool-down routines before or after your time in the water.

For more information on planning an exercise program, refer to the *Personal Fitness* merit badge pamphlet.

The key to a successful exercise program is commitment and consistency. If you regularly complete your full swimming fitness routine three times every week, you will get the most from it. Participating even once a week will make a significant difference. Less than once a week is still better than being a full-time couch potato.

To help yourself make the commitment and develop self-discipline, keep a detailed record of your exercise—how far you swam, time in the water, strokes you used, comparative times, and number of repetitions. These records will chart your progress and show the improvement in your stamina and strength. Seeing your own success will provide even greater incentive.

Swimming Is a Lifetime Skill

Learning to swim a variety of strokes will provide relaxation, fun, and physical conditioning that will benefit you the rest of your life. When the skills acquired through proper instruction and practice are adapted to lifesaving techniques, they can save the lives of swimmers themselves, as well as others. And, of course, swimming at a competitive level is always challenging. Best of all, learning this lifetime skill will leave you with a sense of accomplishment and a fun way to relax with your friends.

Swimming Resources

Scouting Literature

Boy Scout Handbook; Deck of First Aid; Emergency First Aid pocket guide; *Athletics, Emergency Preparedness, First Aid, Lifesaving, Personal Fitness, Sports,* and *Water Sports* merit badge pamphlets

Visit the Boy Scouts of America's official retail Web site at *http://www.scoutstuff.org* for a complete listing of all merit badge pamphlets and other helpful Scouting materials and supplies.

Books

Barsky, Steven M. *The Simple Guide to Snorkeling Fun.* Best Publishing Company, 1999

Colwin, Cecil M. *Breakthrough Swimming.* Human Kinetics, 2002.

Graver, Dennis K. *Scuba Diving.* Human Kinetics, 2003.

Hines, Emmett W. *Fitness Swimming.* Human Kinetics, 1999.

Laughlin, Terry. *Extraordinary Swimming for Every Body.* Total Immersion Swimming, 2006.

———. *Total Immersion: The Revolutionary Way to Swim Better, Faster, and Easier.* Fireside, 2004.

Lenihan, Daniel J. *Underwater Wonders of the National Parks.* Compass America Guides, 1997.

Orr, Dan, and Eric Douglas. *Scuba Diving Safety.* Human Kinetics, 2007.

Thomas, David G. *Swimming: Steps to Success.* Human Kinetics, 2005.

Organizations and Web Sites

American Red Cross
Toll-free telephone: 800-733-2767
Web site: *http://www.redcross.org*

USA Swimming
Web site: *http://www.usaswimming.org*

YMCA of the USA
Telephone: 312-977-0031
Web site: *http://www.ymca.net*

Acknowledgments

The Boy Scouts of America is grateful to Richard Thomas (BSA Aquatics Instructor; director, Aquatics section, National Camping School, Western Region; chair, Aquatics Committee, Grand Canyon Council) for his leadership in coordinating the revision of the *Swimming* merit badge pamphlet and for developing this manuscript. Thanks to BSA Health and Safety Committee members David Bell, Ph.D., for his indispensable assistance with the visuals and text; and to Calvin Banning and Patrick Noack for their input on visuals and text. These devoted volunteers dedicated countless hours to this project. We also appreciate the input and contributions of the following: Lynn Brennard, Albert Cahill, Jay Fox, Bill Hall, Matt Vande Sande, George Troxler, and Steve Terrell.

We thank the Quicklist Consulting Committee of the Association for Library Service to Children, a division of the American Library Association, for its assistance with updating the resources section of this merit badge pamphlet.

The Boy Scouts of America is grateful to the following individuals from the American Red Cross National Headquarters for their assistance: John E. Hendrickson, Program Management and Field Support, Health and Safety Services (and also a member of the BSA Health and Safety Committee), and Mike Espino, manager, Aquatics, Technical Development and Research and Product Development.

Photo and Illustration Credits

©Jupiterimages.com—cover *(mask, snorkel, fins, goggles, stopwatch, butterfly swimmer in background);* pages 6–8 *(all);* 10, 11 *(pool),* 14 *(lifeguard shack),* 65, 67–68, 77, 81, and 94

Wikipedia.org, courtesy—pages 75–76

Wikipedia.org/Mattias Wennström, courtesy—page 79

All other photos and illustrations not mentioned above are the property of or are protected by the Boy Scouts of America.

John McDearmon—cover *(diving illustration);* all illustrations on pages 12, 14, 15–16, 18, 23–27, 31, 33, 36–37, 39, 41, 43–44, 46, 49–50, 56, 69–72, 78, 82–83, 85–87, and 89

Brian Payne–pages 52 and 91